Like Cats and Dogs

Like Cats

**Andrews McMeel
Publishing**

Kansas City

and Dogs

REVEALING YOUR
FELINE OR CANINE SELF

Tanya McKinnon and Gayatri Patnaik

www.andrewsmcmeel.com

98 99 00 01 02 RDC 10 9 8 7 6 5 4 3 2 1

Library of Congress Cataloging-in-Publication Data

McKinnon, Tanya.
    Like cats and dogs: revealing your feline or canine self / Tanya
McKinnon and Gayatri Patnaik.
        p.   cm.
    ISBN 0-8362-5213-6 (hardcover)
        1. Cat owners—Psychology.   2. Dog owners—Psychology.
    3. Cats—Psychology.   4. Dogs—Psychology.   5. Human Behavior.
    I. Patnaik, Gayatri.   II. Title.
SF422.86.M35   1998
156—dc21   97-36975
                                                       CIP

Design by: Lee Fukui

ATTENTION: SCHOOLS AND BUSINESSES

Andrews McMeel books are available at quantity discounts with bulk purchase for educational, business, or sales promotional use. For information, please write to: Special Sales Department, Andrews McMeel Publishing, 4520 Main Street, Kansas City, Missouri 64111.

CONTENTS

Acknowledgments viii

Introduction: A Guide to the Cat, Dog, or Bi-nine Within 1

1. **The Dog Personality** 7
   The Dog Man 14
   The Dog Woman 20
   Case Studies
      Ted: *Reflections of an Unneutered Dog Man* 27
      Janet: *The Tale of a Dog Woman Who Loved Too Much* 33

2. **The Cat Personality** 40
   The Cat Man 47
   The Cat Woman 55
   Case Studies
      John: *An Overly Strategic Cat Man* 63
      Katie: *A Commitment-Phobic Cat Woman* 71

3. **The Bi-nine (Canine and Feline) Personality** 78
   The Bi-nine Man 83

The Bi-nine Woman   90

Case Studies

    Derek: *The Story of a Bi-nine Man*
           Living Betwixt and Between   97

    Chris: *The Saga of a Bi-nine Married to a*
           Cat but Cheating with a Dog!   104

4. Famous Dog, Cat, and Bi-nine People   108

    Hollywood Celebrities   108

    TV Personalities   110

    TV Shows   111

    Celebrity Couples   112

    Famous Interspeciel Couples   113

    Fashion   114

5. Astrology and the Cat, Dog, and Bi-nine Personality   115

6. Common Sense Wisdom for the Cat, Dog, and Bi-nine Personality   197

    All I Really Needed to Know I Learned in the Litter   197

    Chicken Soup for the Bi-nine Soul   201

    Two Stupid Things Felines Do to Mess Up Their Lives   204

    Dogs Are from Pluto, Cats Are from Saturn   210

7. Understanding Your Cat, Dog, or Bi-nine Lover   221

    Understanding Your Dog Lover   222

Understanding Your Cat Lover   226

Understanding Your Bi-nine Lover   231

8. Cat and Dog Breed Preferences   237

9. Paw to Paw: The Path to Interspeciel Harmony:
   Why Can't We All Just Get Along?   243

ACKNOWLEDGMENTS

We would like to acknowledge the generosity, encouragement, and support we received from the following individuals: Sara Baker, Abouali Farmanfarmaian, Christine Fitzmaurice, Anna Ghosh, Martin Goldstein, Sue Hershberger, Dr. Ann Wayne Lucas and the Washington Square Animal Hospital, Hildegard and Alexander McKinnon, Gita Mehta, the Patnaik family, Joanna Pulcini, Martin Quinn-Meyler, Rob Price, Michelle Shinseki, Gloria Watkins, Leah Weatherspoon, William Webb, Sarah M. Zimmerman, the folks at Rob Weisbach Books, and our wonderful canine friend, Zoby.

Neeti Madan at The Charlotte Sheedy Literary Agency has been an extraordinary agent and friend. Finally, we are grateful to Chris Schillig, our editor, for her patience, faith, and vision.

In loving memory of Rande Harvey and Biju Patnaik.

A Guide to the Cat, Dog, or Bi-nine Within

I bet you've never realized that we're in the process of discovering the cat or dog within," Tanya asserted in the midst of a Sunday-night get-together with friends.

"Really?" asked our friend Sara, adding sarcastically, "Is this some new thesis on the mystical connections between animals and people?"

Gayatri, taking another sip of her tea, expanded by saying that every person, without exception, could be categorized as having dog or cat characteristics. Then she issued the challenge: "Describe someone to us in three sentences, and we will tell you if they have a dog or cat personality. We'll also tell you what it means in their romantic and professional relationships if they possess these canine or feline tendencies." And the debate with Sara was on!

In this way we unwittingly hit upon the premise for this book, which proposes that preferring a dog or cat is an act of self-disclosure that can expose both profound and humorous aspects of the human personality. In other words, whether you are a cat owner, dog owner, owner of both, or simply a pet lover, this book explains how these seemingly arbitrary pet choices are far more revealing of your inner nature than you may suspect.

Since the beginning of time there has been an unbridgeable divide between people. Some people insist that race, gender, class, and sexuality are at the root of this divide. We believe there is an infinitely easier way to determine the similarities and irreconcilable differences between people: Read this book and then analyze yourself and your loved ones in terms of their canine, feline, or bi-nine quotient. For instance, are you self-sufficient, tragically hip, and enamored with Robert De Niro or Catherine Deneuve, or are you direct and utterly gregarious with a "thing" for Tom Hanks or Rosie O'Donnell? Perhaps you're enigmatic, feel misunderstood, and relate to Court-

Introduction

ney Love or Dennis Rodman. Read on to find out not only what these important cues are telling the world about your canine, feline, or bi-nine self, but also what it ultimately means about your personality, your hopes and fears, and your aspirations.

Given the age-old fascination with cats and dogs, it no longer suffices to merely understand cats and dogs in themselves. We need a guide for individuals who love and share their lives with these animals. In fact, many a conflict-ridden household could be made more peaceful by answering questions such as the following in an effort to understand the dog-, cat-, or bi-nine–like nature of the inhabitants:

- What happens when two cat personalities live together?
- What are the potential pitfalls when you have a dog personality mother and an adolescent cat personality son?
- What indelible scars are left when the bi-nine personality is forced to live in a dog-centered home?
- Will your dog personality husband ever respond to your catnip fantasies?

Based on our combined thirty-odd years of pet owning, we have decided that it's time to admit that not only do we own the cat and dog without, but also that we harbor the

Like Cats and Dogs

secret feline and canine within. It is intriguing to note that sometimes cat-personality types own dogs to compensate for their more aloof tendencies, while dog personalities may own cats to appear more self-possessed and poised. Curiously, our research has indicated that it is not absolutely necessary to own either animal in order to exhibit the characteristics of either the dog or the cat. All that is required is a willingness to explore one's canine and feline nature in the belief that all humans respond characteristically to these amazing creatures.

Having conducted scores of interviews with cat and dog lovers, as well as with those who are animally challenged, we discovered two vital facts: Anyone, anywhere, at any time, is eager to engage in a conversation about the pros and cons of cat and dog ownership. Secondly, everyone has a strong opinion regarding their pets, which they are longing to articulate. New York City, for instance, is full of adamant cat and dog personalities just waiting for an opportunity to express their feline or canine tendencies, if not the cattiness and hound dog within.

Having trained as cultural anthropologists in the same graduate program, we decided to conduct this study of cat and dog personality traits in humans from a socially scientific perspective. We believe that in the general population there are ways of being, thinking, and acting that reflect certain personality types often associated with animals.

4

Introduction

Consider the articles and books about how "human" animals are, or how their feelings and personalities are similar to ours. What is missing in these studies are the ways in which *people* resemble the household animals they have the most contact with—cats and dogs.

To understand this phenomenon, we began an anthrosociological investigation, frequenting the places where pet lovers congregate such as dog runs, parks, pet stores, dog marathon walks, veterinary offices, and cat or dog grooming and breeding facilities. We approached people, explained our project, and asked if they would mind being interviewed. We spent hours finding out what they thought about themselves, and how they envisioned their own personality in relation to their pets, why they decided on owning a cat, dog, or both, and if they believed that their personality was in any way similar to that of their pets.

It wasn't long before we realized that two species of cat or dog people alone wasn't enough. In fact, there exists a whole network of people who live unacknowledged and unaffirmed in a land of interspeciel limbo—individuals who are both canine and feline at heart, in other words, "bi-nines."

Needless to say, the men and women we interviewed are the people you'll be reading about; they are featured prominently in our case studies but are also included in every facet of this book. In some cases, we use the stories of individuals; in others, we have taken the liberty of creating composites based on several individuals. In all cases, however, we've presented the results of our research in the most straightforward and accessible manner possible. We hope that by presenting you with a clear and concise way of deciphering cat, dog, and bi-nine personalities, you'll become more adept at negotiating, understanding, and exploring that wonderfully teeming cauldron of complexity called humanity.

Once you read this book, dog or cat ownership will no longer seem like a random or whimsical occurrence. So striking are the differences between cat- and dog-like people that acquaintances are made or romantic evenings destroyed based on individuals' attitude toward these animals. You will finally be empowered to discover how your preference for dogs or cats is really giving the world important signals about your feelings toward sex, love, work, family, and friendships. We hope our research will enable you on that compelling path to canine, feline, or bi-nine self-discovery.

CHAPTER I

The Dog Personality

We've all amusingly noted, at one time or another, that dogs and their owners take on an unmistakable, and sometimes even bizarre, resemblance to each other. This phenomenon, although frequently noticed, remains largely inexplicable. We propose a rather simple solution to this conundrum: Usually, people who own dogs have dog personalities, thereby unconsciously choosing the dog that most closely mirrors their inner selves.

Like Cats and Dogs

Dog people in general are expressive, if not sometimes volatile. Larger than life, they give bone-crushing hugs, shriek loudly with laughter or bellow in pain, melodramatic tears flowing from their eyes. **They strive always to live and act decisively in the world, and they succeed in taking life by the horns with tremendous enthusiasm, energy, and unquenchable gusto.**

Unlike their cat counterparts, dog people may appear from the outside as good-natured folks, perhaps lacking in sophistication and subtlety. It is true that dog people, although socially adept, tend to fumble much more in the material world. They are known to trip over nothing, to coordinate a lime-green T-shirt with blue seersucker pants, to overdo the blush, overspray the cologne, and otherwise draw the not-so-uncritical eye of the more fashion-minded among them. However, despite these fashion and etiquette faux pas, no one in the presence of a dog personality can resist such a charming and lovable nature for long. (Well, maybe a cat personality in a crisply starched white Prada summer ensemble.)

But who exactly are dog-personality people anyway? **Essentially, dog people are trustworthy, likable, and utterly gregarious creatures who are beloved by most who meet them.** Frequently exhibiting the most salient characteristics of dogs themselves, dog-personality types strive, in particular, to uphold the ideals of loyalty and friendship. Indeed, when Freud remarked, "Dogs love their friends and bite their enemies," he might as well have been referring explicitly to dog people. If you're fortunate enough to have a dog person as a friend, consider yourself extremely lucky because, once committed to you as a friend or lover, these individuals generally exhibit unswerving devotion and genuine affection. Their loyalty is legion.

Highly nurturing support groups are heavily populated by dog personalities who revel in the social nature of the group and delight in being supportive to their friends. Perhaps as a result of being deeply attuned to their own and others' emotional lives, dog people have a highly developed sense of intuition. For instance, it's not uncommon for them to meet someone new and immediately say, "There's something not right about So-and-so." They are uncannily accurate, so you're advised to listen intently to their gut instinct. Additionally, dog people are renowned for their keen sense of direction and purpose, which means that not only are they driven and goal-oriented at an early age, but they can also find their way home on drunken evenings.

Have we mentioned how ferociously social dog people are? **Find the charismatic core of any party, see how high they score on the "canine quotient," with their**

affability, good-naturedness, and natural charm. These folks love the company of other people, thrive in social settings, and seek communicative and people-based careers. Dog people often become involved in international relations, politics, education, social services, human resources, and even the armed forces—anything that requires organizing and social skills. Given their quick, and often accurate, assessment of human nature, they make effective leaders as well as followers. If you want to organize a cohesive and effective reconnaissance mission, simply put five dog people on a team. They'll intuitively know how to follow a chain of command and get the job done with the least amount of conflict or risk.

Part of their ability to organize and work well in groups is their relatively unconflicted knowledge of themselves as either socially dominant or socially submissive. Obviously, those who are dominant lead, while those who are submissive follow. However, it is a mistake to see one role as being more desirable than another. Interestingly, dog people freely choose to express themselves as being dominant or submissive, and it is not seen as inferior to be at the bottom. At first glance, the submissive dog person may seem meek, but in fact he or she will be acutely attuned to the social dynamics and will often act as a brilliant interpersonal strategist. In other words, these people are able to have their bone and eat it too. The dominant dog personality, on the other hand, is much more overt, intimidating even the most aggressive competitor with piercing eyes, forceful speech, and fierce determination. Indeed, "like a dog with a bone." they are proof of canine tenacity.

The only thing that may jeopardize a dog person's inherent sense of judgment is a traumatic early life. Often, dog people who come from abusive backgrounds continue to suffer a great deal in adulthood. A dampening of spirits in childhood will leave them with a lifelong sense of melancholy, and they'll be less energetic, focused, and athletic than their untraumatized dog counterparts, easily putting on many unwanted pounds if severely depressed. Given the highly sensitive nature of the dog child, early abuse or trauma may lead to overdependency, separation anxiety, and abandonment complexes. For this reason, it becomes crucial that the parents of a dog boy or dog girl take great care to provide them with lots of tender loving care as well as with consistent companionship early in life. It is a fact that the dog personality seldom thrives if deprived of the company of others, and while they occasionally choose to be alone, this is short-lived, often serving some utilitarian function like meeting a deadline or recovering from too much socializing the night before.

Romance is high on the dog person's list, and although the dog personality is well intentioned and fond of per-

Like Cats and Dogs

ceiving themselves as the soul of fidelity, **dog people have an uncontrollable tendency to flirt with everyone who crosses their path.** These folks will chat up airline representatives while buying tickets over the phone, wink at complete strangers across a smoky bar, and strike up intimacies with everyone from the cab driver to their physical trainers. Not surprisingly, one cat woman mother-in-law we interviewed admitted that her dog personality son-in-law flirted with her so outrageously that even she was charmed by the very man she had that morning called "a good-for-nothing, scruffy, unemployed, free-loading musician." Don't bother getting mad; just give in and expect that somehow when you're traveling with a dog person you'll get a free upgrade on US Air, that speeding tickets will be miraculously waived, and that you'll always get the most coveted table in the finest restaurants. No one knows their magic, but they simply work wonders with absolutely everyone. In the final analysis, it appears that dog people truly cannot help themselves: These extroverts simply crave attention.

In terms of love, dog people by and large swear that they're much more serious than their flirtatious character indicates, insisting that they wait a bit longer before consummating a relationship than many people. Perhaps the truth is that while some nonmonogamous and philandering

Dog Personality Characteristics

Tenacious
Extroverted
Friendly
Charismatic
Energetic
Adventurous

Honest
Trustworthy
Flirtatious
Affectionate
Talkative

dog people definitely exist, many dog men and women feel strongly about honoring the integrity of their relationship once they've made a commitment to it.

Keep in mind that the dog personality has a reputation for being the ultimate romantic, seeing sex as an expression of love rather than lust. It must also be remembered that dog people, like their wolf ancestors, more often than not look to mate for life. Indeed, dog men and women have been known to identify the love of their lives within the first twenty-four hours of meeting them. So if the dog person isn't getting real serious with you, chances are he or she may not be planning on keeping their bones buried in your backyard for long.

The Dog Man

Aargh! This dog man, Michael, whom you love, can be so infuriating! He reminds you of your kid brother. Sometimes you want to hug him because he's done something so unexpectedly sweet, and other times you feel like slugging him because he's driving you absolutely crazy. You start to wonder, Is Michael clueless, emotionally dense, or is he just plain emotionally retarded?!

I mean, how could you have misunderstood? He calls you this morning from a pay phone, and although it's hard to hear, it sounds like he's yelling, "Dress up! I'm taking you to the moon tonight! Be ready at eight!"

Anticipating an evening of fine dining, you wear that little black dress—you know the one. You've never had the opportunity to show it off to him before, since his idea of a classy evening is taking you to a hockey or, if you're lucky, a basketball game. But never mind all that now; tonight is destined to be different, you're sure of it. You call your friends, who have (to your irritation) nicknamed him Oscar from *The Odd Couple* on account of his sloppiness, to brag about the transformation.

Eight o'clock finds you pacing nervously in your room; eight-fifteen, and you're fantasizing that he stopped to buy you flowers—you know, to do it right. Now, it's eight-thirty, and you're wondering just how many bouquets he's bringing!

At 8:35, the doorbell rings. You run to the door in anticipation—catching your svelte reflection in the mirror—and you throw it open. Voila! There he is, looking sheepish, garbed in running shorts, a holey tank top, and his favorite rock-climbing shoes. Instead of flowers, Michael's holding out a rope for you. You have some idea what you'd like to do with it.

"What are *you* all decked out for?!" Michael exclaims. "Where'd you think we were going anyway?" he adds, starting to laugh. You're pissed off now, so angry, in fact, that you can't talk. Suddenly wondering if he's done something very wrong, Michael looks a bit bewildered, then tries quickly to atone. "No, you look really...sexy...much better than when you wear sweatpants. I mean, not that you look absolutely awful in those sweatpants or anything...."

Then Michael just stops talking, and you have to admit you're grateful for that. Enveloping you in a loving hug, he engages you with a warm open-mouthed smile, and you feel your anger melting away. Well, you've stopped expecting a Prince Charming transformation to occur, but it no longer matters. You've found someone infinitely better, a man you can trust because he's not trying to impress you, someone who is earthy, real, and wonderfully alive. And then you understand. All this time, Michael's been trying to surprise you with a special rock-climbing trip by the light of the full moon and suddenly you can't imagine any-place you'd rather be.

Does this sound like anyone you know? A lover, a brother, a close friend maybe? It's the essence of the dog man—no double-talk, subtlety, or innuendo here, just a well-meaning, but sometimes completely clueless, hunk of a man. Walt Whitman was unknowingly describing a dog man when he said he intended to "sound his barbaric yawp o'er the rooftops of the world." Yelling "seize the day" with abandon, the dog man succeeds in overcoming all obstacles with tremendous exuberance and energy. Although the world may initially attempt to trounce his happy-go-lucky nature, the world has something important to learn about him: **Dog men have extraordinary resilience and amazing recuperative ability. A dog man doesn't intend to be down for long.** The dog man's motto gives us insight into the essence of his person-ality. "If I fail at something, it will only increase my desire to attain it. And it will make my success all the sweeter." Tenacious to the core, he will ferociously, if not stubbornly, work at something until he has gotten it absolutely right.

It comes as no surprise that the dog man is generally externally motivated, and that he tends to measure suc-cess by what he has achieved in the world. Indeed, the antithesis of the dog man is Rodin's famous sculpture of

The Dog Personality

The Thinker. In other words, rarely is the dog man a dreamer or a philosopher, rather he is a doer, a creator who relishes hard work and clearly defined goals. He'll happily, and often innovatively, initiate pretty much anything but keep in mind that the details or the fine-tuning will be left to a fastidious cat person.

Thriving in careers where they can attract attention, be in the public eye, be communicators, or have the opportunity to travel, dog men often choose careers as professors, actors, journalists, soldiers, politicians, pilots, travel agents, or train conductors. However, dog men would do well to remember that their careers must reflect not only their freedom-loving personality, but also their unique goals, otherwise they'll undoubtedly experience depression, physical lassitude, and tremendous mental stress. Doing a job that he doesn't believe in or working where he can't express himself openly will cause the dog man to feel that he's living a lie. And he abhors lies.

Individualistic and expressive, dog men have the uncanny ability to generate enthusiasm for any venture, no matter how odd sounding. Does anyone you know want to lead a dog sled team through Alaska in the dead of winter? Maybe the plans include taking a hot air balloon around the world when the dog sled mission is completed, and he's hoping you'll join him? These plans have Dog Man written all over them, and the only one who'll readily accompany him is a—you guessed it—dog woman. It is vital to a dog man's well-being to have a challenge, and this takes a physical, mental, or even an emotional form. You'll see a droop in their tails, a dullness in their usually sparkling eyes, and a general hang-dog expression in a dog man who's not challenged. Indeed, unhappiness always takes a physical toll, probably because his body and his mind tend to be very connected.

He's physically active, guileless, and carefree; who wouldn't want a dog man around? Well, of course, there is the question of his tact—or the lack thereof. Dog men need to be trained not to put their paw in their mouth. Don't laugh, this may be harder than you think. As bizarre as it seems, you must often explain to dog men, in painstaking detail, why the following would be inappropriate: "Wow! You look so much better in this dress than the other one. That one really makes your butt look wide and kind of weird!" Or how about this one that we recently overheard in the midst of a crowded wedding. "Jill! Is that you? You look terrific. Meet my friend Max. Say, have you gained weight? I hardly would have noticed except—" When you stop smiling, he will innocently wonder what happened, until Max leads him aside and attempts to explain his latest faux pas to him. (Believe it or not, he really did think you looked terrific. It was just that he hadn't quite expected to see a more voluptuous you.)

Dog Man Characteristics

Determined	Tactless
Outgoing	Good-natured
Open	Loyal
Expressive	Gregarious
Enthusiastic	Sloppy

Another frequent complaint about dog men is that they're not always the best listeners. It's not that they do it on purpose, but their minds somehow just wander away from the topic at hand while they mentally organize their next project, camping trip, or vacation. One cat woman we interviewed, Emily, was particularly annoyed by this characteristic in her husband and revealed her special tactic for getting his attention. "Honey, did you hear about that scandal involving that famous football player in the NFL, now, what's his name?" (Yes, it worked like a charm.)

Faults notwithstanding, your dog man—so full of exuberance, plans, and energy—is a special person. Truman once remarked, "If you want a friend in Washington, get a dog." We modify this to read, "If you want a friend or lover for life, find a dog person." As a friend, he's fiercely loyal and generous; as a lover, he'll fill your world with warmth and love; and as a father, he's extremely protective and caring. Even if you don't manage to nip all his flaws in the bud, you can rest assured, you've snagged the pick of the litter. Guaranteed.

The Dog Woman

She's an enigma, this dog woman of yours. You just can't figure her out. Sometimes she seems so incredibly worldly, tough, and together, and then other times you swear you're with the most delicate, sentimental, and naive person in the entire world. You have to wonder if she herself understands this paradox.

Probably not, actually, and you should know that she prefers it that way. You may have noticed that she's not the most introspective person you know, and she's not interested in merging the differing aspects of her personality to form a cohesive whole just so *you* can understand her. If you don't like it, fair enough, but don't even try to demand something of her that she doesn't demand of herself. It simply won't work.

So, the question remains, Why are you still so intrigued? We'll alleviate your misery by telling you: **No matter how hard you try, you'll never be able to predict fully what this woman will do, how she will**

The Dog Personality

act, or what she will say next. Essentially, this mystery is what draws you to her. The funny thing is that you're not only drawn to her physically, but you're also compelled on a mental and spiritual level. While you'll never be able to figure the dog woman out in all her complexity, this section will help you get a general idea about this charismatic woman you've fallen in love with, are related to, or are friends with.

Outgoing, energetic, and always fun to be with, the dog woman is a lover of adventure and new experiences. With a tendency to be gung ho about life and love, she sometimes gets hurt due to her own naïveté. She can be amazingly sentimental and will fall for tear-jerker movies every single time, gushing away right next to you. But don't assume for one second that you're dealing with a weak woman; on the contrary, this is one of the toughest people you'll ever meet.

Like the dog man, she is very well intentioned but equally tactless, and almost always blunt. Consider a dog woman—Michelle—whom we interviewed at the dalmatian walk in Manhattan this year. Michelle was convinced that the local sauna would be a great place to set two of her friends up on a blind date. "Why not?" she rationalized, when a few of her friends looked appalled and quickly vetoed her idea. "They'll both see what they're getting into, and what a great way for them to break the ice! Or, in this case, the sweat." Getting excited, Michelle added, "And, hey, if they don't like each other, there'll be plenty of other people to meet! Oh, isn't this perfect?...Why are you guys looking at me like that?" As with the dog man, explaining to her why this scenario might be inappropriate for a blind date will be a challenge, to say the least.

Careerwise she will gravitate to many of the same high-profile jobs as her male counterpart. As long as she can communicate—through teaching, counseling, writing, translating (as at the United Nations), or prosecuting—she will feel fulfilled. She has a special affinity for jobs involving travel and loves nothing more than a frequent change of scenery. Therefore, many dog women are attracted to foreign postings or work as war correspondents, international journalists, and Peace Corps volunteers. As long as she is challenged mentally, she will excel at her work. Otherwise, signs of discontentment and ultimately depression will show on her face, will be evident in her energy level, and will even be apparent in her body language. Long-term depression, as you might suspect, has physically and emotionally debilitating repercussions for her.

The dog woman, usually attractive in an earthy way, prides herself on her high level of physical fitness. She's not one for caking on the makeup. While she might apply some lipstick, foundation, and eyeliner for evenings out, she definitely prefers the natural look at

The Dog Personality

work. Not one to lounge in expensive silks like the cat woman, this pragmatic canine dresses for comfort first and style second. Still, what's interesting about the dog woman is that wherever she goes, she can't help but attract attention. And she usually doesn't even have to try—something about her very naturalness is refreshing and charming to everyone she meets. It must be said, however, that this effervescent woman can be an outrageous flirt, and some might find her loud, even raunchy. The truth is that often she is just trying to have a good time. She's certainly not "easy" and might be annoyed that you assumed she wanted to go home with you. So what if she was sitting on your lap. Can't a woman just horse around without it being a big deal? What's a lively girl to do anyway?

Although this woman wounds the male ego on a regular basis, she does so without malice and with such innocence that you can't help but forgive her. You should keep in mind that she's not one to hide her emotions, and if she's feeling something, you'll definitely know about it. This isn't someone who will manipulate or hide anything from you; she has no interest in games, and you had better not be playing any either or she'll give you a pretty nasty bite before she eliminates you from her busy social calendar, and, believe us, that will be your loss.

When it comes to romance, a big hurdle for the dog woman is discerning the difference between someone who would be a good friend and someone who'd make an ideal lover. Part of the reason she's misunderstood is because she can be confused by what she wants in an intimate relationship. She can, in fact, be easily taken advantage of, especially as a young woman, because of her trusting nature, but we don't recommend preying on her naïveté. You see, when she finds out—no matter how much you apologize—the friendship or love relationship will be over *for good* because you've done the one thing she can't forgive: You've knowingly (and irrevocably) broken her trust.

Trust and loyalty are the cornerstones of the dog woman's personality as well as her relationships. Although deeply social, she abhors shallow friendships and meaningless social encounters. Her motto is, Let the cat people network, dog people just wanna' have fun. We say, make a dog woman friend and have a friend for life. We know two best friends, Sheila and Wendy, who met on a sixteen-hour layover in Nairobi, and although one lives in Seattle and the other in New Orleans, they have sustained the intimacy of their initial bond for twelve years. Now that's dog women for you. You might also be warned that dog women have been known to sacrifice lovers who threaten their close friendships, as well as sacrifice friends who they feel wrongly disapprove of their lovers. These women choose their loved ones first and everyone else a distant second. On the whole, dog

Dog Woman Characteristics

Persevering	Tactless
Social	Genuine
Warm	Nurturing
Dynamic	Naive
Direct	Sentimental

women tend to be realistic in assessing the weaknesses of their friends and loved ones. So, think twice before asking your best dog woman friend what she really thinks, and if you don't really want a blunt and candid answer, please don't ask!

But let's face it, if you broke up with your lover on Monday, and your boss fired you on Tuesday, come Wednesday there is no better place to go for chicken soup, understanding, love, and inspiration than the house of your dog woman friend. By Friday she'll have found you a date, job possibilities, and a couple of things you hadn't even realized you needed. This is precisely when you will sit back, confident that when all is said and done, nothing compares to the true-blue friendship of a dog woman.

Like Cats and Dogs

As a mother, dog women show their real pack instinct. It would be incorrect to say that dog women coddle their children but let's just say they are *very* involved in the little critters' activities. They believe that it's vital for their children to experience a variety of pastimes so they will probably take one child to soccer practice, another to band practice, one to theater rehearsal, and the last one to the chess finals. We know one highly accomplished dog mother who underwent no fewer than three major career changes in order to accommodate the demanding schedule of her children's academic and extracurricular activities.

Show us a child actor, a professional gymnast, or a teen model, and we'll show you a loving and driven dog mom. Take Brooke Shields. Would she have gotten so far without the tireless encouragement and support of her dog mom? Interestingly enough, no matter how hard dog moms push, their kids rarely seem to resent them for long. Maybe that's because these wonderful women enter their children's world. Toddlers relate to them as playmates, adolescents see them as confidants, and adult children simply refer to them as their best friend. Perhaps the secret lies in the dog mother's credo, Children first, second, and third.

Honest to the core, ruthlessly blunt, and a passionate hater of all duplicity, the dog woman finds it difficult to "lie" to her kids about the most innocuous things, even where babies come from. Although a dog father would indulge their stork fantasies, she will reason that if they are interested enough to ask, then they should be prepared for the truth.

This brings us to the question of her sometimes brutal honesty. Please don't ask her opinion of something unless you want the honest-to-goodness truth. If you're sensitive about starting to bald and ask her if it looks bad, she will reply, "Of course not, Charlie Brown, I could hardly even tell!" Now, you may not understand this at the time, but what she means is that, well, yes, you are losing a little hair. but she believes you look as handsome as ever. It may get tiresome translating these seeming insults on a regular basis, and you can speak to her about her tactlessness, but be patient! Delicacies are simply not, nor will they ever be, her strong suit. She is not for the fainthearted or for overly sensitive types, but if you desire a strong, adventurous, honest friend or lover full of surprises and warmth, look no further than the dog woman.

CASE STUDIES

TED:
Reflections of an Unneutered Dog Man

This story was told to us during a taped interview, and we felt, due to the compelling nature of the material, it should remain in the first person.

Like Cats and Dogs

Stephanie, my older sister whom I adore, is a classic cat woman, and while there's nothing wrong with that per se, I myself am strictly a dog man. I want you to be clear about that right off because when she and I start fighting, as the cliché goes, like cats and dogs, you'll understand why.

For instance, the other evening I overheard Stephanie cattily gossiping about me to her friend Kim. I couldn't make out that much at first, but it sounded as though Kim was telling Stephanie that she had a crush on me. I was glad to hear that since Kim is really pretty, but I honestly wasn't too surprised—girls seem to fall for me all the time. And then Stephanie said, "Not again! Why is it that *every* time a friend of mine meets Ted, she *has* to have a crush on him. Look, I love my brother and all, but—"

"But...what's he really like?" pursued Kim eagerly. "He seems so perfect for me. He's adventurous, loves to travel, is outgoing, really friendly, definitely attractive, a consummate athlete, and—"

"Yeah, yeah," interrupted Stephanie, "stop with the laundry list. We all know he's a typical dog person, and I agree he has all those great qualities. It's just that...Oh, what's the point...All right, you want to know what Ted is really like, I'll tell you: Take John F. Kennedy's preference for blond bombshells, add a pinch of James Bond's charm, a tablespoon of Jack Nicholson's bad boy persona, then add a heaping cup of Henry Miller's feral sexuality, and top it off with a very, and I do mean *very*, generous helping of Warren Beatty's arrogance...and what do you get?"

"What?" asked Kim, puzzled. I was bewildered myself and had an uneasy feeling.

"You get the womanizer to top all womanizers—in other words, my brother, Ted. Boy, is he a dog man who needs to be neutered!"

Both Kim and my sister burst into raucous laughter. I no longer wanted to listen; talk of castration isn't really my scene.

After Kim left, I accosted Stephanie. Since dog people can't successfully hide their feelings (unlike their sly cat counterparts), I told her I had heard everything and felt angry and betrayed but, most of all, grossly misunderstood. For once, we decided to have a mature and dignified debate about this whole subject of me supposedly being a "womanizer," or as Stephanie likes to say, "an unneutered personality."

I said, "Okay, Steph, I have to tell you before we start that I'm tired of all this feminist castration stuff, and all I want to do is tell you my side of the story. And, for once, please just try to hear what I'm saying! First of all, I'm just going to flat out admit it, and I'm sure I speak for all womanizers when I say that we adore beautiful women. There's nothing better in this world than seeing a gorgeous woman walk down the street. No, I correct myself, the only thing better than seeing her walk down the street is having that woman on your arm. I like being seen with them, holding them, possessing them, and—"

"What?" screeched Stephanie. "Did you actually say 'possessing them'? Okay, you know, I was kind of joking about you being a womanizer but now you're..." Stephanie saw me breaking into a hearty laugh and realized I had added the last part just to get her goat.

"Like I was saying, before I was so rudely interrupted," I continued nonplussed. "There's nothing wrong with appreciating beauty in this world. Now, if I lied to a woman when I was dating her, that would be wrong but I've never done that."

Stephanie rolled her eyes disbelievingly. "You've never lied to a woman? You make Dick Morris look like a Boy Scout! How can you say that?"

"Steph, I'm serious. I've never said to any woman I've been with that I wanted to be monogamous. I take the advice of Jack Nicholson, a ladies' man extraordinaire, who wisely said, "I never commit past dinner!"

"Look, little brother, I'm going to tell you something. And whether you're technically having an affair or not is beside the point. You don't commit—past dinner, as you so glibly say—because you *can't*. Flitting around from one woman to another, treating women as if they're simply the flavor of the month, is just an easy out, a way of never committing fully to anything. The tragedy will be years from now when you finally meet someone special. Look," she added softly, "I just think you might be very lonely someday."

I didn't know what to say to that, but it didn't matter since that was the end of our conversation. Me, lonely? Ridiculous! Years have gone by since that talk, and I'm happy to report that I've been with numerous women and haven't had the urge to settle down even once. It's funny, but I called Stephanie the other day and reminded her how she had once compared me to the supposedly great womanizers, like Kennedy, Nicholson, and Beatty, and we laughed when I said, "You know, I was so irritated at the time, but I should have just thanked you for including me in such distinguished company!" Always an older sister, Stephanie said she still worries about me.

Then the strangest thing happened: I met this woman, Julie. I don't know what it is about her, but I think for the first time in my life, at the age of thirty-eight, I'm finally ready to commit. We started dating, and I've honestly never felt more fulfilled. But after a while, there was a little problem. You see, I wanted to be with Julie, I really did, but I couldn't seem to control my urges. I mean, it's like trying to stop smoking cold turkey when you've been smoking two packs a day for twenty years!

Like Cats and Dogs

I didn't know what to do. I loved Julie and there was no one I've ever desired more, no person I've ever respected more. I thought about my options: I could cheat on her. Even thinking about that made me feel bad. I mean, she really deserved so much more. Then again, if I didn't cheat, I'd have to suggest having an open relationship, and I know she'd be appalled by that idea.

Well, after much internal debate, I decided not to tell her anything. I did my best to be faithful, knowing that cheating would jeopardize our relationship, but I just couldn't stop. Then I established guidelines never to do it in town where I could be seen, but I knew that Julie would eventually find out anyway. After three years, she finally did; then she left me for good. I was crushed.

I've never talked to my sister about this again, but if I did, I know exactly what I'd say. You see, people think that womanizers are selfish and make women feel cheap, like conquests or something, and there's some truth in that, though that's never been my intent. These women who feel betrayed are allowed to express their rage and frustration and are fully justified in saying we're cads, and everyone agrees with them. But for us so-called womanizers, we never really stop paying the price of our own infidelity. I'm not trying to say we deserve sympathy or anything, but the sometimes brutal loneliness that just creeps up on you can feel absolutely devastating, and that's when you realize how alone you are. Steph's prophesies had come true after all. Here I was with no one to confide in and no one to go home to.

As a young man, I fancied myself a smooth ladies' man. Years later, I was shocked to realize that I'd become a sex addict, but I couldn't stop, the perks were too good. Only after many years have I been able to accept the truth of this life that I've created: Being an "unneutered personality," as Steph would say—with all its breathtaking highs and crushing lows—is simply an unalterable fact of my existence.

JANET:
The Tale of a Dog Woman
Who Loved Too Much

"And I...will always love you-ooooh..." crooned Janet so grossly off-key that strangers in the bar offered to buy her drinks if only she would stop singing. Over the last two hours Janet had gone from being lightheaded and giggly, to tipsy and flirtatious, to full-fledged drunk. Todd and Amy knew what was next: Janet would soon be in full-confessional mode and they would be forced to endure yet another monologue about Tony, the man Janet was currently dating. Much to Janet's distress, their relationship was crumbling fast.

"I just don't get it," blubbered Janet. "I mean, I try so hard in a relationship, and it's like...I don't know what goes wrong."

Janet's lower lip started quivering uncontrollably as Todd put his arm around her and gently said, "Maybe you try *too* hard. You scare people off, you try to be so good and so perfect that...well..."

"That you drive people crazy!" finished Amy, clearly the less subtle of the two.

"But how can you not try hard? Isn't that the point of being in a relationship?" asked Janet, puzzled.

"Janet, of course you're supposed to try hard, but it's almost as though you love too much, if you know what I mean," explained Todd. "Yeah, that's it. You're a classic dog person who loves too much for her own good."

"You're absolutely right, Todd!" exclaimed Amy. "I never thought about it that way before, but that's exactly what's going on!"

"What are you two talking about?" muttered a thoroughly confused Janet. "I thought *I* was supposed to be the drunk one, and now my two best friends call me a dog. Thanks a lot."

"We're not calling you a dog, Janet. We're saying you're a typical dog person, who is loyal, good-natured, and sentimental," said Todd.

The Dog Personality

"Yeah," added Amy, "and since you tend to wear your heart on your sleeve, you get hurt often. You invest in relationships too fast and then are devastated when some guy you barely know breaks your heart. It's like you're starved for affection or something."

"Look," replied Janet, clearly irritated, "I am most definitely *not* starved for love, but I want you to know that this has been really terrific for my self-esteem. I mean, first I was a dog, and now I'm a dog starving for love. Well, all I have to say is 'woof' to you guys."

Janet started barking like a dog, much to Todd and Amy's amusement. The bartender happened to notice and remarked, "Well, it sure beats her singing, doesn't it?!" Laughing, everyone agreed.

Janet was known as being attractive, exceptionally bright, outgoing, and quite the "catch" in her college circle. However, she frequently had trouble deciding whether a person she liked was better as a friend or lover.

In spite of being popular, Janet, like many of us, had lingering insecurities that became obvious in her love relationships. As Todd and Amy had observed, Janet repeatedly tried too hard, loved too much, and invested emotionally in relationships way too fast. What was harder to see, however, was the reason Janet overcompensated: She was terrified that she wouldn't be appreciated for her real self. The reasons for this were, of course, complex, but in part they could be traced to a classic dog woman's being raised in a perfectionist cat-centered household: She never felt she could express her true identity. To please her parents, Janet unconsciously began mimicking how they acted, a pattern that continued with her lovers. Instead of communicating her true feelings and ideas, she pretended that things were always just fine.

Take her relationship with Tony, for instance. Tony and Janet had been friends for six months. They moved in the same social circle, and everyone around them thought they would make the ideal couple. Soon Janet began to believe it too. So when Tony asked her out, she agreed, determined to make what everyone thought was the perfect relationship on the outside, the perfect relationship on the inside as well.

However, it was obvious within the first four weeks that although Tony liked the idea of a girlfriend, he was not emotionally mature enough to handle a relationship. He rarely invited her out with his friends, frequently stood her up, and was late for everything they did together. If the truth be told, they shared little in common apart from a few friends. However, Janet felt too nervous to have an honest conversation with Tony about their differences. When she did see him, rather than initiate a disagreement by voicing her anger, she tried harder to seem interested in him and his hobbies.

The Dog Personality

The minute Janet became romantically involved, she felt desperate to be perfect, exactly as she had with her parents. It didn't matter how late Tony was or how often he was disrespectful of her. After two months, Janet was already psychologically invested in the relationship, not because she was convinced Tony was the one for her, but because she was afraid that if the relationship dissolved, she'd be alone.

One evening, in particular, stood out for her. She had planned an intimate three-month anniversary surprise dinner for Tony and had asked him as a special favor to arrive at her place at eight o'clock sharp. As usual, Tony got caught up in an early evening basketball game and completely lost track of time. By the time he arrived, he was an hour late, as well as sweaty and dirty. But instead of honestly communicating her feelings to Tony, she sat through dinner resentfully while he acted as if nothing were amiss.

Pained by her situation, her friend Todd gently took her aside. "You're angry at Tony, Janet, but, most of all, you're angry that your relationship isn't working out. Can you admit it and just let it go?"

"Oh, Todd, of course I'm not angry at Tony," she said.

"Well, you've sounded pretty resentful over the last couple of weeks."

"Look, I suppose I've been upset but it's not about Tony, it's about me. I think if I just work at it harder, be better, then it could all work out."

Like Cats and Dogs

"Janet," Todd said slowly, "it's not a matter of you trying harder. We both know that's not the point. What I'm trying to say is that you're withholding vital emotional information from Tony, and without communicating this, you'll never function effectively within any relationship. You need to tell him that things aren't working, that you're angry."

Janet had stopped speaking. She felt her bluff being called and hated how it made her feel. Although she rebuffed Todd's remarks, she couldn't stop thinking how right he was. She realized how she always allowed herself to be compromised in relationships and that she had a habit of picking totally incompatible men to date. Most of all, she saw how she set herself up for failure time and again.

Suddenly, Janet realized that she had to stop living this lie; she wanted to claim her real identity. She started by accepting Tony as a friend instead of a lover and was amazed to see that by honestly communicating her feelings, she and Tony were able to be closer, in many ways, than they had been while dating. Afterward Janet didn't grow desperate to start dating again, as she once had. She surprised everyone by planning an exciting trip around the world. When she returned ten months later, Janet was an altogether new woman. Todd, Tony, and Amy couldn't get over the transformation—she seemed so amazingly comfortable with herself.

The Dog Personality

Janet used to believe that if she wasn't who her parents or lovers wanted her to be, that she wouldn't be loved. One afternoon, she and Todd discussed at length how ironic it was that she had adapted her personality to suit others, but then felt upset when they didn't appreciate the real her. It was a self-defeating and vicious cycle that Janet had begun to change. It felt good. So good that she started a successful peer counseling group in college later that semester.

Exactly one year after breaking up with Tony, Janet started dating Todd. Having gotten closer and closer over the months, they realized their feelings for each other were deeper than those of friendship. His openness and warmth enabled her to continue growing in surprising ways, while Todd was rejuvenated by Janet's vibrancy and newfound honesty.

At a surprise birthday party for Janet, Todd and Amy presented her with a new fangled CD player with an elaborate karaoke system built in. The card read, "You've come a long way, baby! Everything is getting better and better about you except for your singing!" Janet thought back to their conversation in the bar a year earlier and smiled. She *had* come a long way. She grabbed the karaoke mike, dedicated a song to Todd and Amy, and started croaking away.

CHAPTER 2

The Cat Personality

Whoever first said, "Curiosity killed the cat," must have been living with a cat person at the time. Deeply curious, cat people are obsessed with wanting to know what makes things tick. Stemming from an intense desire to uncover the "why" of things, cat children may take apart the radio, overwind watches, remove the heads of dolls, or keep elaborate insect farms. Later in life, this curiosity is transformed into a keen ability to problem-solve in any area that interests them. This fixation, we might add, does not stop with animate objects.

The Cat Personality

Just consider famous cat sleuths like Sherlock Holmes and Hercule Poirot. Deeply introspective, cat people pride themselves on being able to analyze and articulate their deepest thoughts and feelings. As any Woody Allen film demonstrates, cat people willingly go to therapy in order to more deeply explore the complexities of their intricate psyches. **It is a rare cat person, indeed, who does not manifest a deep and abiding interest in the workings of the human mind.**

Cat people are fascinating, yet paradoxical, creatures. A typical cat person can seem intoxicated with you one moment, then shrug and walk away with cool indifference the next. As anyone who's lived with one of these inscrutable creatures must know, felines are reserved, holding themselves at a slight distance from the turmoil of everyday life. Circumscribed and slightly internal by nature, cat people like to have their space and enjoy it too. In many households, the extent to which a cat person will go to for solitude and privacy is lore. In fact, it is crucial to a cat person's sanity to periodically withdraw from the pressures and demands of everyday life. Without this precious time alone, which is as vital to a cat person as air is to the rest of us, these poor creatures will begin to feel overwhelmed, burdened, and yes, even catty.

Psychologically healthy cat people are restrained, difficult to understand, and very much in control of their emotions. Frequently accused of being inscrutable, these people are masters at bluffing. Remember, too, that these people rarely explode with violence, but when they do—watch out: Pushed to the edge, a cat person will go for the jugular, using piercing intelligence to overwhelm even the most intimidating adversary. Despite the lore of "cat fights," real cats fight paw to paw only rarely, choosing instead to find high ground and bluff. So too with cat people who are living embodiments of the strategy, A strong offense makes the best defense.

Interestingly, when bad things happen, these people have a profound ability to land on their feet. As opposed to the helpmate nature of every dog person, cat people seldom offer unsolicited advice out of respect for the privacy they demand in return. In fact, cat people are notorious for retreating and licking their wounds in private. They like to go inside themselves using their keen analytic ability to help them recover. Indeed, this self-sufficiency is one reason they've earned the reputation for having nine lives.

In terms of physicality, cat people are extremely fun loving, playful, and prone to acting as the trickster in a group. These people are graceful and light-footed with sharp reflexes—except perhaps, when under the influence of their favorite catnip substance. They tend to pursue sports such as gymnastics, dance, rock climbing, ice skating, squash, and the martial arts. If not physically active themselves, they have a deep appreciation for activities that require precision, skill, and coordination. In fact, cat people frequently use their keen analytical skills as spectators and make great referees, judges, and sports commentators.

In line with their appreciation of athletic grace and coordination goes their love of beauty. Cat people possess a keen aesthetic eye and choose either the most modern or the most classically understated clothing and furniture. Cat people can't help themselves; they have a slight disdain for the unstructured and earthy ways of their dog neighbors. Spilled food, Birkenstocks, sweatpants, and tennis shoes are definitely distasteful to the cat sensibility.

When it comes to careers, cat people tend to be highly successful as investment bankers, accountants, corporate and tax lawyers, editors, and artists—not to mention, winning poker players. Fiercely competitive, cat people are guarded about their ideas and possessions and driven by an almost unparalleled work ethic. In most cases, cat people like to work individually, pushing the envelope of their resourcefulness and talent, to the delight of any boss. (Although, bear in mind, they usually are the boss or work alone.) Cat people can become completely engrossed in their work, sometimes forgoing hours, days, or even weeks of familial or romantic contact as they push to meet a deadline or complete a masterpiece. However, the same holds true for their leisure time. When they play, they play hard, loved ones and kids will then receive their undivided attention. As you can well imagine, cat people tend to get what they want. Not all of them measure success in monetary terms, however. Whatever their goal, cat people will meet and surpass it in the course of their career.

For those of you involved with a cat personality, it is vital to realize that you may never completely know or possess this man or woman because of the cats' unequivocal need for privacy even from the people closest to them. In addition, the cat personality is characterized by a deepseated desire to explore or wander, and this is true both literally and figuratively. Indeed, the authentic cat personality will revolt if not allowed total freedom. As you may suspect, this has been known to cause more than a few rifts in the otherwise smooth course of true love. Neither will they put up with being romantically neglected, abused, or disrespected. No doubt about it; if your cat lover is not treated with respect, he or she will be out of there in two shakes of a feline tail.

There are, however, cat people (slightly on the neurotic side) who, for whatever reason, have had their more independent nature curtailed in kittenhood. These people fre-

Cat Personality Characteristics

Curious
Competitive
Reserved
Inscrutable
Internal
Intellectual

Artistic
Self-sufficient
Disciplined
Strategic
Fastidious

quently appear much more dependent than their better adjusted counterparts. Occasionally, these individuals are even mistaken for dog people. However, just spend enough time with them, and you'll see their back arch and their eyes narrow while they pounce dramatically on whatever has caught their attention. Who knows, it could very well be your current girlfriend or boyfriend.

This brings us to the issue of sexuality. **Let us simply say, cat people are the absolute masters of seduction.** Slightly vain, cat people are meticulous about their ap-pearance—young or old, they make sure that their wardrobe is always in impeccable condition. When these people initiate a seduction, you'll be swept off your feet for the duration of their amorous attentions. Seduction is a slow and sensual art form for the cat person. From candlelit dinners to warm, cozy fireside snuggling, the cat person luxuriates in the art of erotic foreplay. However, beware! Cat people, if not completely smitten with your every move, can be easily distracted after the consummation of your long, smoldering sexual tension. Not to mention, many cat men and women, before being struck by the urge to nest permanently, amuse themselves by seducing people for sport. Now this may sound a bit cruel, but it's not really. Cat people like a challenge, romantic ones in particular. So just make sure your cat person is planning to catnap for the long haul before you pick out the chinaware.

Oh, and one more word of caution about your cat Casanova. Even if your cat person is quite smitten with you, they tend to be very wary of individuals who seek commitment too quickly. Should a cat person sense your investment in them is deepening too quickly, you may trigger their feline claustrophobia response. Our advice, once you've been swept off your feet by a sultry cat woman or a debonair cat man, is to take it easy for a while and see just what this man or woman's intentions really are. If nothing else, your reserve is bound to both intrigue and heighten their amorous interest in you!

The Cat Personality

The Cat Man

The cat man is nothing if not passionately interested in life. He is insatiably curious about the inner workings of both inanimate and animate objects. Since childhood he's been reading nature books, building complicated airplane models, and perhaps even reading a little Freud on the side while the other kids can't even spell Oedipus complex. Just look at any cat man's college transcript. Whether he's an engineer or a political science major, he'll have managed to take enough psychology courses to constitute a minor.

Of the many skills in the cat man's repertoire, it must be said that careful listening ranks among the top three, along with a love of seduction and a keen analytical ability. Quite frankly, when it comes to listening, understanding, and sympathizing, the cat man is unparalleled. Need we say more than Freud was a cat man? Not only will the cat man give you a willing, nonjudgmental, and sympathetic ear to speak into, but once you've unburdened yourself, he will happily assist you with any dilemma. You might say the cat man is a born problem solver and is certainly enamored of puzzles. Just take Sean Connery in Alfred Hitchcock's film *Marnie*. The primary reason for Tippi Hedren's appeal for Connery, apart from those nifty little two-piece suits, is the psychological mystery of her compulsive stealing. Connery is so intrigued that he marries her to solve the puzzle. **As Tippy found out, when a cat man wants to understand you, you have never been so understood!**

However, we do offer a minor word of warning when it comes to these charming and seductive listeners. Perhaps you saw John Malkovich's performance in *Dangerous Liaisons*? Well, never has there been such an honest portrayal of a cat man gone awry. Along with their unusually high intelligence and keen information-gathering skills, these felines are also known for their more strategic and, at times, even controlling side. As Malkovich demonstrates in his seduction of Michelle Pfeiffer's character, puzzles are not the only games that intrigue cat men. They are natural-born hunters and thrive on the chase, making seduction a favorite pastime. **The combination of sensitivity, emotional perceptiveness, and highly controlled emotionality make them some of the most accomplished womanizers.**

As most people who've been seduced by a cat man will tell you, there is nothing quite like the experience. He may send you three dozen long-stemmed red roses on Monday, and then not call till Sunday. A close friend of ours, a cat woman psychoanalyst named Audrey, told us about a classic cat man—Matthew—whom she dated, and gave us this helpful synopsis. We remembered it well, and, should you date a cat man yourself, we advise you to keep it in mind.

Matthew appeared at Audrey's apartment one Friday evening with a bucket of champagne and two first-class tickets to Bermuda. After a heavenly weekend, he surprised Audrey again the following weekend by whisking her off for a secluded tryst at his cozy log cabin in the woods. However, after these two blissful weekends, Matthew abruptly informed Audrey that he had ultimately decided to marry another woman the following week. Audrey couldn't have been more shocked; not only was she unaware that Matthew had been seeing other women, but she had no idea that he was serious enough to marry someone else. Fortunately, Audrey is a classic cat woman herself and got her composure back fast enough to send Matthew's bride her sincere condolences.

It's not that these men are inherently mean-spirited (although a small percent of them could rightly be accused of being genuinely cruel); it's just their feline nature kicking in. The cat man, for all his good points, and there are so many, is also known for his general ruthlessness and strategic emotional withholding. More than his dog or bi-nine counterpart, this man understands the effect his words and moods can have on others. And we'd just like to mention that artistic cat men have a tendency to, shall we say, excessive moodiness. Take for example one of his darker moods, in which he'll sweetly notice how terrific you look while commenting that you seem to have lost weight. Just as you beam with appreciation, he'll suddenly icily suggest you keep those five pounds off for good. Naturally, even the most composed individual could become angered by such brazen emotional manipulation. We advise that when you find your cat man in these moods, either fight fire with fire or ignore him completely until his sunnier, more attentive, and genuinely flattering side resurfaces—and it will.

But let's not get too distracted by the cat man's darker nature. He does, after all, have so many charming and wonderful qualities that serve to make him such a complex character. Take for example his healing qualities. More than a few women we interviewed spoke repeatedly of how the cat men in their lives had helped them through a difficult time by listening intently and compassionately. One woman in particular, Holly, confided to us that she had grown up in a severely dysfunctional and abusive household. Soon after meeting her cat boyfriend, Ed, she was able to cry and grieve for the first time. In her words, "Ed was able to really empathize with me and always loved me exactly for who I am. He's helped me recover my inner child and has enabled me to grow both individually and in the relationship." So it should come as no surprise that a disproportionate number of therapists and counselors are cat men.

As we've said before, the cat man loves to be challenged intellectually. Consequently, you'll find cat men psychoanalysts, CIA agents, and all forms of artists, especially in film, photography, painting, and sculpture. These men love creativity and cherish the ability to express their unique world vision. One cat man we interviewed works as a freelance writer and adjunct professor by day, while sculpting, painting, and writing poetry at night. He recently had his first small gallery show, and not surprisingly, all his pieces sold. In a nutshell, there are no artistic or intellectual limits for this creative soul.

When it comes to money, cat men are usually not driven to extremes. You'll find him at times generous and usually farsighted in terms of investment possibilities such as real estate. **The cat man likes money but often won't compromise his genuine interests for the sake of making it.** Fortunately, he's so clever, disciplined, and strategic that money usually accrues from whatever he takes seriously.

In sports, this man, as in everything else, is motivated to play positions and games that require strategy. These men love chess, backgammon, or bridge, as well as all forms of martial arts and racquet sports. In contact sports you'll find them playing the position of quarterback, pitcher, or center. The truth is that this man won't feel like he's had a full workout unless both his mind and body have been utilized. Unlike dog men, cat men tend not to go in for extreme sports, but when they do, it usually takes the form of rock climbing, mountain climbing, or glider flying.

In their friendships, this man is capable of genuine and caring connections. Sometimes these men prefer the company of dog women for their greater ability to emote and because of their less guarded and more honest natures. However, cat men can be boys with the best of them, and although they don't usually make a habit of the more outlandish and loud forms of male bonding, come the Super Bowl or the NBA playoffs, watch out! You'll find them lining bar stools in your local sports pub right along with their canine and bi-nine brethren. And apart from the cat men's analytical comments, you won't be able to tell any of them apart.

No cat man profile would be complete without some mention of those men whose fastidiousness has garnered them international recognition. None more famously personified than neurotic and compulsively neat Felix Ungar of *The Odd Couple*. Surprisingly enough, however, only about 20 percent of cat men we interviewed displayed such an overt need to have "a place for everything and everything in its place." As a rule, cat men, like cat women, are usually emotionally inscrutable and composed. If they are neat, and cat men do like things to be orderly, it's usually because they love to be in control of their surroundings.

If the cat man has one Achilles' heel, however, it is bound to be his complicated relationship with his mother, which is crucial to know for those interested in seriously pursuing a cat man. It's not clear exactly why relationships between cat men and their mothers, especially those who are dog women, tend to be so intense, volatile, and ultimately unresolvable, but that's the way it is. Most cat men raised by dog mothers spend a great deal of time trying to escape the warm and well-guarded litter she's so successfully created. They find innovative ways of staying out past dinner and breaking curfews—some even manage to join the Red Cross in Afghanistan! While there are no lengths too great for the cat man to go when it comes to escaping his mother, don't be deceived for a minute: The cat man, far from wanting to flee, is secretly thrilled that no matter how far he runs, his mother will inevitably reach out to find him. Is it any surprise that this man's favorite childhood game was hide and seek, and his favorite playmate (although he'd never admit it) was Mom.

Therefore, it comes as no surprise that the cat man's most treasured secret is that no one will ever take his mother's place. Even as he virulently complains about her intrusiveness, her nosiness, her constant nagging, and her tendency to turn up uninvited to see if

Cat Man
Characteristics

Attentive   Devoted
Analytical   Successful
Seductive   Motivated
Charming   Strategic
Moody   Able to solve problems

he's done his laundry, in his heart of hearts there's no one he'd rather see. Now let's not get confused, the cat man is genuinely self-sufficient and maddeningly aloof, but when it comes to escaping the madding crowd his most favorite place of respite is, you guessed it, Mom's. When you do eventually end up setting up house with this man, it might serve you well to remember that outright competition with your mother-in-law is a game you cannot win. He will, unfortunately, allow his mother to subtly criticize you, and when she reminds him that his old room at home is always waiting, just ignore her. It's just her way of rekindling that mother-son bond. In fact, complaints about mom will fall on deaf, if not unfriendly, ears. The golden rule is that he can criticize his mother but you can't. The best tactic here is simply to smile tightly and wait for the little bundle of frenetic in-law energy to go home. Hopefully, there'll be at least a state or two between you and her, making frequent visits difficult. Just remember, he's loyal to you; it's just that he was loyal to her first!

The Cat Woman

The cat woman is the most private person you will ever meet. Exuding a sense of quiet mystery, it is important for anyone who knows one of these exotic women to remember: **Just when you think you know what a cat woman is going to do, you don't!**

It would be a mistake to say you can't get to know a cat woman. Instead let us suggest to you how elusive she is. This woman will slip through your fingers and through any net you lay out to catch her. We've often suspected that the sirens, those beautiful seducers of sailors in Greek mythology, must have been a slew of felines.

The cat woman, like Kathleen Turner in *Body Heat*, is the epitome of calm, cool, and collected. Since she reveals nothing she doesn't want you to know, it's almost impossible to figure out what she's thinking, so don't waste your time and energy trying.

Like their cat brethren, cat women are extraordinarily intelligent, sporting keen analytical abilities and insatiable curiosity. Find a cat woman in any setting, and she'll be the one who's privy to everyone's secrets. People naturally trust this reserved woman and seek out her objective advice, especially when it comes to affairs of the heart, where, we'll have you know, she's an absolute pro.

Cat women are experts in the art of seduction; in fact, they wrote the handbook. But let's take a closer look at this seductive breed. These women tend to come in two varieties. The first is embodied by Sharon Stone's elusive and provocative character in *Basic Instinct*. This kind of cat woman will knock your socks off at first glance. She oozes sexuality, whether she's disheveled or perfectly groomed. One glance from her and your knees will turn to Jell-O. We once read an article by a supermodel who complained that men just wouldn't ask her out. The interviewer cynically jibed her for this, but we just nodded our heads. The sad fact is that some cat women are so stunning that the poor things inadvertently frighten admirers off. Men frequently think these women would never go out with "someone like them" and consequently don't even approach this unique woman. Instead, they mosey over to the slightly disheveled dog woman, drinking beer with her work buddies and talking up a storm.

It's at times like this that the cat woman's inscrutability becomes a liability. We offer cat women a word of advice: You've got to give the rest of us some encouragement. We don't all share your impenetrable facade, and sometimes

we're a little intimidated. But before we get too busy feeling sorry for this feline, let's remember that these skillful
creatures have, over the centuries, adapted and perfected
the art of pursuing—without appearing to look even mildly interested. Once a cat woman has set you in her sights,
you'll be amazed at how quickly you end up at her
doorstep with a bouquet of roses, and when she reveals the
truth years later, you'll swear she wasn't even interested in
you at the time. Or was she? **One reason they're so
successful at getting what they want without
appearing to try is because cat women possess an
uncanny power of suggestion.** A cat woman might
walk into your office, casually strike up a conversation
about the ballet, and somehow within a week you'll be
asking her to the Bolshoi, if not trying to fly her to St.
Petersburg, the moon, and wherever else she wants to go.
These women, for all their aloofness, are, as the song goes,
"simply irresistible."

The second type of cat woman you may encounter is a
bit less flashy. She may be your co-worker, the one in the
conservative blue suit with her hair pulled tightly back.
However, make no mistake, these women who appear
downright Victorian have the power to take you by surprise. You may have worked with her for months, and perhaps felt intellectually intimidated by her—after all she's
considered the top in her field and graduated summa cum

laude from Georgetown University—when one day you come into the office, and wham! You're swooning. We call their appeal slow motion, since it may take you a bit longer to become smitten but, we assure you, that it's no less intoxicating than the more overtly sensual cat woman.

It may seem indelicate to say this, but the simple truth is that **cat women are enamored of sex and sexuality, period.** One poor bi-nine we interviewed secretly confessed that his cat woman girlfriend was just wearing him out. We weren't surprised. Curiosity is not the only thing these felines are insatiable about.

But enough about sex, let's talk about another equally potent facet of the cat woman personality: her temper. You may just have gotten to know a cat woman and cannot fathom what we mean when we insist that this sensual, purring creature has a temper. Well, consider yourself duly warned! The cat woman will say *anything* in a fight. She will hit you below the belt, and anywhere else you might feel vulnerable. All her usual diplomacy and social skills will evaporate, only to be replaced with something akin to the wrath of Attila the Hun.

One fight will be enough to keep you battle weary and cautious for quite some time. Most people will either leave in the midst of such an explosion or learn to apologize before she hits a full boil. The dangerous exception to this rule takes place when a strategic cat man sets his sights on her as a challenge. Their relationship, as you can imagine, becomes something like a fearful reenactment of *Who's Afraid of Virginia Woolf*, with each party verbally outsparring and outmaneuvering the other in an endless battle of wits. We usually recommend that these cat men and cat women stay clear of one another, and seek out a more even-tempered bi-nine or canine companion, if not for their own sake, then for us innocent bystanders.

Keep in mind, too, that the cat woman may tire of many things quickly, but vengeance is not one of them. Consequently, we suggest that whether or not you are on intimate terms with a cat woman, it's best not to make her your adversary since she will patiently wait for the opportunity to pay you back tenfold. We interviewed a cat woman, Laurie, who told us she was betrayed by her co-worker and, after waiting four years, was in a position to terminate this individual's career. Now, we're not trying to frighten you, we just believe you should think twice before carelessly getting on her bad side.

However, it's only fair to balance this dark side of her personality by promising that if you are one of the few people a cat woman comes to truly love, admire, respect, or simply like, then you have made a tremendously powerful ally. Cat women usually have one best friend whom they cherish for a lifetime, a few close friends whom they keep equally long, and many business associates whose careers they have actively advanced. Having a cat woman on your side can be a life-changing, not to mention potentially lucrative, experience. Just ask anyone who has started a business with a cat woman.

Along with their loyalty in friendship comes their devotion as mothers. Unlike dog mothers, cat moms are a bit less overprotective. Cat mothers keep a close eye on their babes—woe to anyone who'd try to harm her kittens—yet they prefer to remain at arm's length. Often they'll allow the little ones to touch a relatively warm stove, to chase a skunk, or otherwise get into things enough to discourage repetition. In other words, cat mothers tend to warn once and then let life take its course. It's no secret that her children usually learn self-sufficiency and self-control somewhere between standing and potty training.

One odd quirk of the cat woman is that she can be taken in by gimmicks. Because the cat woman prefers the path of least resistance, she sometimes likes to do things the easiest way possible. So, if you've ever wondered who actually buys those sweater knitting machines on the infomercial channels, you can bet it's a devoted cat mother, angling to knit all four of her kids' sweaters by Christmas.

When it comes to their careers, solitude is golden. Cat women insist on working alone and often run their own businesses or work as artists, academics, photographers, or freelancers. When you do find them in larger organizational structures, it's usually as the boss. As you may have noticed, cat women have a deep-seated aversion to being told what to do. While they're not the most overtly sociable people in a group, they certainly are the most people savvy, and it is precisely this talent that gives them their keen ability to get promoted. Should you find yourself working under a cat woman, be grateful; she's a real gem. Believe it or not, these seemingly **reserved and perfection-oriented women can also be great mentors and team leaders** since they seem to have a knack for inspiring the creative best in the people around them.

Cat women also tend to be acutely aware of their image. If they do achieve celebrity, they will, in all likelihood, be extremely media averse although aware of their media persona and style. Take Audrey Hepburn and Grace Kelly as typical cat women celebrities; they were supremely dignified and classically elegant in public yet spent a great deal of time avoiding the limelight. They will definitely avoid generating a cult of personality like Madonna because **even fame cannot shake the cat woman's primal need for privacy.**

Some cat women who work and live alone can take self-sufficiency to an extreme. Consequently, one does find more homebodies among cat women than among any other group. Usually, these women allow their intellectual life to take complete precedence over their bodies.

Cat Woman
Characteristics

Private

Unpredictable

Sexy

Sensual

Professional

Spontaneous

Tasteful

Understated

Provocative

Ambitious

Trustworthy

We might also add that the cat woman is the most high-maintenance breed in the kennel of life. Not only is she psychologically complex, but she revels in her own complexity. Some cat women will spend hours leading you down blind emotional alleys and up steep affective hills while you get to know them. Okay, so the cat woman can be a bit selfish, or, shall we say, self-involved, when she's in one of her introspective moods. In this case she'll demand your attention but will blithely ignore you at the same time. This may be initially frustrating, but remember that if you ignore *her* for a while, she'll soon turn that piercing gaze your way, and demand to know what's so interesting over there in your world.

The Cat Personality

The cat woman will be the first to admit it; she loves gifts. You can't go wrong buying her chocolates, champagne, roses, perfume, diamonds—the bigger the better. Keep in mind, however, that she's not a crass materialist but a sensualist with extraordinarily good taste. This is a woman who is not afraid to pamper herself or be pampered and will indulge herself at ski resorts and spas, insisting on monthly massages, pedicures, manicures, and facials. Even if she dresses simply for work, rest assured; she treasures her monthly visits to the beauty parlor and spending a whole Saturday preparing to slip into that little black dress for a night on the town with you.

CASE STUDIES

JOHN
An Overly Strategic Cat Man

"Love is not a chess game," Jennifer shot back before she stormed out of the apartment, slamming the door behind her.

For the first time in a long time, John felt helpless. And John had structured his entire life around never having to feel helpless.

In high school, he had been one of the most popular boys and not only because he was captain of the tennis team. At sixteen, he had strategically planned his high school career, his after-school activities, his courses, the type of car he would drive, and even the doomed Ska band he would start in order to gain a certain hip status. John relished mental challenges; he loved being the improbable candidate who succeeded not through brawn but through brain power. Tall and lean, John was an unlikely candidate for many of the things he had already accomplished in his life.

Accepted into a prestigious university, he double majored in psychology and economics, garnering distinction in both fields. In his personal life he felt equally victorious. During the first month of his freshman year he identified one of the most attractive and accomplished women on campus, a junior named Dionne, and was dating her by the end of the year. His roommate, a reclusive engineer, was in awe of him and referred to him as "a real player." John's relationship with Dionne secured his standing with the most sought-after people on campus, and her graduation left him the most eligible bachelor around.

Entering his junior year, John was just where he had planned to be. He was class president, respected by his professors, envied by his peers, desired by numerous women on campus, and known as the most likely candidate for a summer internship on Wall Street. John saw life as a game, and so far he was winning.

The Cat Personality

Uncertain of how to succeed in business, John saw his summer internship as the means to clear up his confusion. Identifying the general director with whom he had the most in common, John spent the summer strategically allying himself with this man's team. He mastered all his tasks and even managed to become an indispensable researcher on a big-money deal his boss was overseeing. He also developed a relationship with the company's senior partner, Mr. Radcliffe. John became knowledgeable about Radcliffe's hobbies, his favorite stocks, vacation spots, and cigars. In short, he studied every facet of this man, and his shrewd strategizing paid off by the end of the summer when Mr. Radcliffe invited him to enter business school as a future employee of the firm.

John was ecstatic. On the trading floor he could merge his keen analytic prowess with his love of risk while simultaneously making a fortune. He was twenty years old and believed there was no person he could not charm, no deal he could not close.

During his senior year in college, John continued to excel academically and pursued only the women who seemed disinterested in him or unattainable. As he told his male friends, "I just don't like to do anything that isn't a challenge." Slowly, he developed a reputation for being a heartbreaker. As he told one accusatory girlfriend, "It isn't that I don't care for you. It's just that the sparks aren't quite the same as they were in the beginning." Needless to say, she and quite a few other women were not on speaking terms with him by the end of college.

However, despite this minor romantic turbulence, John was on top of the world. He graduated summa cum laude, was accepted to one of the highest-profile business schools in the country, managing to excel there in the same way he had in college. By the time he graduated with an MBA, he was already an indispensable part of Radcliffe's investment banking firm and a formidable trader on "The Street." Unlike his friends at business school, he exchanged his hat and gown for a vice presidency at this company. He was twenty-four years old and he felt invincible, every gamble he had taken so far had paid off tenfold.

Acclimating quickly to the lifestyle of a big-money trader, John sported one of the most impressive client lists in town, frequently wooing even the most loyal clients from other houses to the amazement of his colleagues and rivals. Meanwhile, he continued to cultivate his intimacy with Radcliffe as if it were a carefully manicured garden. Convinced that such careful planning would ensure that someday "all this would be his," he believed his seemingly grandiose expectations were, in fact, rooted in reality.

It wasn't long before Radcliffe bestowed the kiss of unrivaled favor upon John by inviting him to spend the

The Cat Personality

holidays in Paris. John was overcome with joy. Here was the moment when all his dreams would unfurl in planned procession before him. He canceled everything and everyone on his calendar, giving Radcliffe an unequivocal and heartfelt yes.

On the plane ride over, John took inventory of his life, patting himself on the back for each of his strategic successes—Dionne, the class presidency, Radcliffe, and his latest high-profile client. They had all been winning moves on the chessboard of John's life.

John arrived in Paris to find all of Radcliffe's immediate family gathered, with the exception of his oldest daughter, Jennifer. She was studying art at the Sorbonne and would not be able to join them until she was satisfied with the sculpture she was currently working on. John paid her much-discussed absence no mind as he, in turn, charmed Mr. Radcliffe's mother, his wife, their son, and their youngest daughter, Amy.

Rising early on Christmas morning, John wandered into the kitchen for a cup of coffee. There he found an indescribably attractive young woman arranging flowers on the table. He was so struck by her open and sensual face that for a moment he simply stared at her, mesmerized. She smiled and asked if she could help him with anything. Recovering himself, he looked at her more closely—she was wearing an apron over her jeans and T-shirt. Surely this must be one of the maids, he thought, and after giving her his breakfast order, retreated into the living room where he found Mr. Radcliffe poring over the morning newspaper. When the young woman in question entered with John's breakfast, Mr. Radcliffe appeared startled.

John, uncertain of what this meant, took the tray, dismissing the woman with a nod of his head. To his surprise, instead of returning to the kitchen, she strode over to Mr. Radcliffe, removed the paper from his hands, and threw herself on the couch opposite John. It was John's turn to look visibly shaken. Mr. Radcliffe cleared his throat and politely inquired, "Do you two know each other?" With a sinking feeling in the pit of his stomach, he watched as the young woman leaned over and, with a mischievous gleam in her eyes, said, "Hi, I'm Jennifer, you must work for my father."

It was the first time in a decade that John was at a loss for words, thought, or strategy. Slowly, there spread over him the most delicious feeling of provocation. Finally, he thought, the ultimate challenge. Jennifer, looking into his intelligent brown eyes, secretly felt an equal thrill.

The rest of John's vacation was spent pursuing the elusive Jennifer all over Paris. He sent her flowers, which she threw out with the evening trash, and gourmet treats, which she fed to her puppy. One night he waited for her outside her school until midnight, but she, fully aware of his agenda, chose to work on her sculpture all night long.

The Cat Personality

It seemed that no matter what he did, Jennifer was one step ahead of him. At last, John cornered her on the way to her room one night.

"I'm going back to New York tomorrow, and I was hoping we could have a farewell dinner." He could see a frown fleeting across her face and decided that perhaps withdrawal was a better tactic than the tireless admirer routine had been.

"Well," she hesitated, "I guess a farewell dinner would be okay."

John thought, Checkmate.

At dinner, John was surprised by how forthcoming and relaxed he felt, in fact, he didn't strategize for at least two hours. It seemed Jennifer had an equally good time, since she ended the evening by encouraging him to stay for two extra days. The two extra days turned into a week as they drove all over the French countryside. Finally, their vacation had to end, and John reluctantly left.

Back in New York, John mulled the situation over. On the one hand, surprisingly enough, he really did care for Jennifer. Still, he couldn't help thinking how being married to her would speed his career along. The only obstacle he foresaw was her unpredictability and complete independence—he had to consider that she might not be willing to get married, and he prepared to do some pretty fast talking.

When Jennifer came to visit John in New York, she sensed the change. He was attentive, but there seemed to be a deeper current of concentration in his mindfulness of her. Her cat woman senses hit the red-alert button. A deft game player herself, Jennifer knew when she was being manipulated, but rather than flee, as she usually did when she smelled a rat, or in this case another cat, she owned up to her feelings, deciding to have an honest talk with him.

"John," she began that evening, "I really like you, but in order for us to be close, we can't keep playing these silly cat-and-mouse games with each other."

John's eyes narrowed—she had confessed first so the advantage was his. He took his time to answer. Jennifer noted how much he looked like a cat about to pounce, and sighed. She had dated two other ambitious cat men, and each time it was the same: They chose winning over love.

Slowly, John began to weave his tale of adoration, waxing eloquent about a future with her. But something was wrong, Jennifer seemed unmoved. Instead of moving closer, she withdrew! "Look, John," she repeated with exasperation, "I've been here before, and I know exactly what game you're playing. But I'm not a stepping-stone in your career or a challenge or anything else. Either you love me for me, or we just can't be together."

John sat back impressed, reassessing his options. This was becoming the most exciting game he'd ever played. He decided to go with a psychoanalytic reversal. "It seems like *you're* the one caught up in games."

The Cat Personality

"John," she said with an air of finality, "I'm trying to say I care about you, and if you care about me, you'll drop the act and just be with me."

She was good, this girl of his, he thought, deciding to go all out with the innocent act. Looking her dead in the eyes he said, "I honestly don't know *what* you're talking about, sweetheart."

To his amazement, Jennifer stood up abruptly and announced, "Love is not a chess game, John," and stormed out of the apartment—and out of his life—forever.

KATIE
A Commitment-Phobic Cat Woman

This story was told to us during a taped interview, and we felt, due to the compelling nature of the material, it should remain in the first person.

She was tall and slim with a breathtakingly beautiful face and short glossy black hair. I think everyone's mouth just kind of dropped open when she walked into the business meeting. I mean, she couldn't have been more than twenty-nine years old, and here she was strolling into a potentially multimillion-dollar deal in jeans and a blazer. She had just expanded her designer line of clothing, and our firm had been hired by a larger corporation to make her an offer. I have to admit I don't remember much about business that day. She was so poised and confident, yet so funny and gracious, I must have fallen in love with her the minute I saw her. Even after rejecting our best offer, we all had an amicable lunch. To this day, I've never met a woman who matches her dynamism.

To my mind, Katie was ideal: young, career-oriented, savvy, successful, and independent, she was in a league of her own, establishing her own rules and making everyone play by them. For months, I tried hard to impress her, and I guess I finally succeeded when she laughingly accepted my dinner invitation.

Looking back, I should have seen the warning signs. She rescheduled the dinner twice at the last minute. Right then and there, I should have known that work was her number one priority. But I was too thankful she could squeeze me into her busy schedule to notice those small telltale signs.

What can I say? Dinner was fantastic. She was everything I had dreamed about and more. We discovered we shared similar interests in art and music and were both avid cross-country skiers. What excited me most was her air of, not indifference, but coolness, like she knew my game, and it didn't impress her one bit.

Those first few weeks with her were the most exhilarating and terrifying of my life. Every time I saw her, I felt like I was about to hang glide off a sheer cliff, and to be

The Cat Personality

honest, no one has ever made me feel that way again. We went skiing, ate at fabulous restaurants, went to art galleries, and made love about a bizillion times.

Six months later, we had our first mini-crisis. We were spending more than half our time together, and one night after a romantic dinner I surprised myself by saying, "Look, let's just get married!"

Well, you would've thought I'd just shot her cat. Katie went pale and started to stutter. I'd never seen her lose her composure like that before. She started saying things like, "But Paul, we really haven't known each other that long." And, "But I thought we were both career focused; I don't really understand where this is coming from."

You could have knocked me over with a feather. Here I was thinking of honeymoon locations, and she was saying we didn't really know each other! We spent the next two hours alternately arguing and apologizing. But the end result was her call: no marriage, but we could try living together after a year.

I was hurt, but I convinced myself that she was right. We had the rest of our lives, so why rush in? I reasoned that once we'd lived together for a while, marriage would be a natural next step. I made a commitment to increasing her sense of security with me, and convinced myself that I loved Katie precisely *because* she wasn't trying to maneuver me into marriage.

Like Cats and Dogs

Time passed, we moved in together, and things were blissful. I felt a greater sense of security, as if we were really in it together. Yet it was odd; the more secure I felt, the more irritated and irritable Katie seemed. I remember one night in particular. I came home cranky and began complaining to her about my back aching and having to deal with a difficult client. Katie interrupted me and said angrily, "Oh, stop whining like a baby! I'm not your mother, for God's sake."

I was stunned. All I wanted was for her to be on my side, to be supportive when I felt vulnerable, but that seemed to go against her very nature. In fact, my being vulnerable seemed to threaten her. I felt humiliated, angry at being made to feel like a clingy child. Here I was, trying to be sensitive, and I actually felt guilty for having my own needs. The more I thought about it, the more I realized Katie didn't seem to need anyone, and to top it off, she didn't like to be needed. It's strange how life works out.

And when it came to money, I had always been the primary provider in my other relationships. But if I paid for something, Katie made it seem like a crime. I was trapping her, curtailing her precious sense of freedom.

I could sense the insecurity growing inside of me. I started feeling like I had nothing to offer her, emotionally or materially. One night I finally had enough and began screaming, "Lie to me, please, Katie, just lie to me! For once, just tell me I'm the greatest man in the world, or at least that I'm special!" Katie must have seen the desperation on my face, but would you believe she didn't give an inch? She coolly informed me she was tired of my tantrums, and then returned to her office to work late.

I had reached the end of my tether. I didn't want autonomy, career-obsession, and composure anymore. I just wanted a woman who made me feel needed and important—a little larger than life, if you know what I mean. Even today, I see that fight as a turning point and suspect that I unconsciously unlocked the door of infidelity that night. I kept reaching out to Katie, but she kept thwarting any possibility of intimacy, so I eventually stopped trying.

I'd never cheated before, but that evening I needed someone. I called the only person I thought would understand, Lynn. Lynn and I had been working together on a project for months, and I had thought of her as a buddy, my office confidant. As I told her my story, she made sympathetic noises and offered to venture out into the cold to buy me a beer. "A few beers will make anything seem better," she joked. I confess, a few beers did allow me to see Lynn in a whole new light. Our affair began that very night.

At first, I rationalized the affair by telling myself that Katie had made me insecure and that I needed to be with someone who stroked my ego. After two months, it was obvious both to me and to Lynn that something had to give. So, I told Katie.

She was understandably livid at first, and then she was just very hurt. Katie said she felt betrayed and blamed me for insisting we live together so soon. "I could have spared myself all this pain if I had just followed my own instincts and not yours," she said sadly.

Part of me agreed. *I* was the one who had pressured her, and now here I was, knocking the vessel of our relationship against the rocks. As the mist of her anger cleared, I asked her if she still loved me, and she replied she did. I knew I still cared for Katie deeply and that the affair with Lynn had been a cowardly way out. After terminating the affair, I suggested that we give couples' therapy a try.

In therapy I finally told Katie, and myself, the truth. I didn't want a submissive wife who cleaned house while I earned the bacon. I loved Katie because she was the opposite of that, but I also had to admit that I wanted her to have moments of weakness, neediness, and dependency just like I did. Katie's unwillingness to give me that made me feel so inadequate and helpless, as if I were doing something to be ashamed of. Then one day in therapy, Katie turned to me and simply said, "Let's face it, Paul, I guess I'm just commitment phobic."

Once she said that, lights started going off in my head. As she talked about the importance of her career and of how ambivalent she was about having kids or getting stuck in a dead-end marriage as her mother did, a lot of her behavior began to make sense. She finished by saying how misunderstood she felt and started to cry. It was one of the only times I'd ever seen Katie break down, and my anger toward her vanished at that moment.

I realized Katie wasn't purposely trying to hurt me or make me feel inadequate, she just couldn't give me what she felt unentitled to herself. We stayed in therapy for several more months, slowly learning to tell each other how we really felt about things. Unfortunately, our relationship ended in spite of our efforts. My idea of a relationship is all about bridging spaces, and Katie's is all about preserving them. We loved each other but we were at an impasse.

There is, however, a bright side to this story. I slowly got over Katie and ended up falling in love with, and marrying, a commitment-positive dog person like myself. Katie, on the other hand, remained single, tirelessly expanding her company. But a couple of months ago, Katie called to tell me she'd met someone, a man who even reminded her a little bit of me in some ways.

"He's a highly successful photojournalist," she gushed, "so he's only in town about one week out of every month."

We both started laughing, and I said in all sincerity, "Well, Katie, this could be the one you've been waiting for!"

CHAPTER 3

The Bi-nine
(Canine and Feline)
Personality

What do Virginia Woolf and Dennis Rodman have in common, apart from being tremendously gifted? You guessed it—they're classic bi-nines. **Indeed, it may be convincingly argued that the bi-nine personality is the most enigmatic and the most misunderstood of our three personalities.**

But who or what exactly are these fascinating creatures? First of all, pragmatically speaking, bi-nines are people who either own cats and dogs at different times in their lives or have owned cats and dogs simultaneously. Also, the term bi-nine is frequently used to describe those individuals for whom the labels "cat person" or "dog person" seem insufficient. **Secondly, these individuals are nonconformists, iconoclasts, and idealists in the truest senses of these words, and they adamantly refuse to be bound by society's norms or by stuffy and stagnant tradition.** They pride themselves on being different, and if they had a theme song, it would absolutely have to be Sid Vicious's unique rendition of "I Did It My Way."

Bi-nine people of any age and every culture are invariably progressive and open-minded. They often live their lives pushing the envelope of tolerance in relation to themselves, others, and the causes they believe in. Notorious for their support of the underdog (or undercat), these people are highly sensitive and sometimes even persecuted for their beliefs. They tend to approach life from a both/and rather than an either/or perspective. These trailblazers seek unity among diversity and excel in unstructured environments. Although their unconventional outlook often makes them resistant to the daily grind that the rest of us must bear, they are by no means unsuccessful in life. Consider, for instance, the fame and fortune attained by such bi-nines as RuPaul or Sandra Bernhard.

Like Cats and Dogs

As a result of the bi-nine disdain for the nine-to-five routine, some dog and cat people disparagingly label bi-nines as being irresponsible, unfocused, and perpetually confused, but the bi-nine will refute these accusations, declaring that they have never and will never desire society's approval. It is true, especially later in life, that bi-nines tend to be very comfortable with themselves, believing that imposing societal labels on their complex inner reality limits their potential.

Not infrequently, the intelligence, passion, and idealism of a bi-nine personality becomes twisted by deep depression. Many sensitive bi-nines, in fact, become misguided as a result of being brutalized by the rigid norms of a predominantly cat-and-dog society. Consequently, many bi-nines may go through a horribly cynical and bitingly sarcastic phase, which is ultimately an elaborate mask to hide their inner pain. These bi-nines tend never to achieve their full potential since they are stunted by the cat(ty) and dog(matic) absolutism surrounding them. Like Kurt Cobain (bi-nine poster boy, if ever there was one), bi-nines have a tendency toward excessive substance abuse as a way of coping with society's rampant misreading of their true personalities. And if the depression runs too deep or continues for too long, these sensitive creatures might resort to suicide or might die an unnatural death as River Phoenix did.

The Bi-nine Personality

Effective communicators, philosophers, musicians, and, interestingly enough, psychics, bi-nine personalities often gravitate to the theater since acting allows them to explore their multifaceted identity in an innovative way. Their exploratory nature and nonjudgmental attitude make them impressive peacemakers, mediators, therapists, and all-around healers. The *Star Trek* search for "new frontiers where no man [or woman, presumably] had ever gone before" could be conducted only by a crew of bi-nines.

Obsessed with extrasensory perception, paranormal phenomenon, astrology, and the like, bonafide bi-nines will swear that Agent Fox Mulder of the *X-Files* was created in their mold. While they are fond of Scully (a cat person), they envision Mulder as the bi-nine's pajamas, and see themselves as living a similar kind of semipersecuted life. Constantly seeking to map the uncharted territory of their inner psyches, bi-nines will go on retreat to ashrams in India, monasteries in Tibet, and to healers in Africa. They are frequently spiritual and most comfortable with nondenominational philosophies, although they do have a penchant for such Eastern religions as Hinduism, Buddhism, and Taoism.

The persecution complex of many bi-nines brings us to a rather unsavory point: While bi-nines can be generous and fair, their selflessness can border on—how shall we

Bi-nine Personality Characteristics

Paradoxical	Progressive
Precocious	Idealistic
Centered	Unconventional
Complex	Abstruse
Misunderstood	Evolved
Unique	Eccentric

say it—the insufferable. To elaborate, bi-nines, not infrequently, appear to have an interesting combination of a superiority complex and a martyr complex. They have been known to look down on those who are less "evolved" (their favorite word) than themselves. After all, it's hard to be expansive, visionary, and centered while the rest of humanity struggles with the mundane aspects of a humdrum existence like cleaning the bathroom, taking out the trash, or subduing heartburn.

Finally, in terms of love and romance, the sky is the absolute limit with the bi-nine. Whether you are an aloof cat person or a gregarious dog person, chances are that you will be able to come to an elevated understanding with a bi-nine. The only thing that the bi-nine requires to be

The Bi-nine Personality

happy in a relationship is to be heard and respected, period. You have to remember that the bi-nine holds nothing sacred and is simply irrepressible. Consequently, the best thing you can do is to enjoy the ride and know that you'll never forget it. If you attempt to curtail the bi-nine, he or she will either commit emotional suicide or turn completely away from you—forever. Leashes just aren't their style! If these basic qualifications are met, bi-nines will prove to be romantic, poetic, and utterly devoted to the art of sexuality. **These seductive creatures have usually mastered the *Kama Sutra* and are probably pioneering their own forms of sexual intoxication as we speak.** If you've ever harbored sexual fantasies, which you've been too embarrassed to try, you better believe that any bi-nine worth his/her nine characteristics will give you the thrill of your life.

The Bi-nine Man

At thirteen, James was seen as an oddity. He'd skipped a couple grades; he was fluent in Italian, Japanese, and Swahili; he was a member of Mensa, and he had an extraordinarily dry wit. Both men and women were attracted to this slim-hipped wiry young man who was highly intelligent, wildly idealistic, and fascinated by all aspects of the unknown. It was his interest in Eastern religion, African art, and all paranormal and metaphysical activity that proved most intriguing to those around him. They were simultaneously intrigued and intimidated by it all. What no one suspected, though, was how deeply alienated and alone James felt.

Ah, the bi-nine man—enigmatic and precocious, unconventional and progressive, misunderstood and lonely—there's no one quite like him. He scares you with his intensity and extreme moodiness, but, like a moth to flame, you can't help being attracted. You've tried to break down the intricacy of his character and make sense of him, but he's so much more complicated than the sum of his parts.

There was his incredible knowledge of Eastern religion and Greek and Roman mythology, for example. Even as a boy he devoured books on classical mythology as if he were reading comic books. In the midst of a mundane discussion about cartoon characters, he would suddenly make some parallel about how Spiderman is really a manifestation of Arachne, the Greek mortal who was turned into a spider, and how fascinating it is that certain tropes of existence always seem to compel humankind. The kids at the lunch table would glance at each other a little surprised, not knowing quite how to respond. All they'd been doing was chatting about which cartoon characters were their favorite, and then this guy had to say something so...well, weird. Why did he do it anyway? Was he socially dysfunctional—a show-off, maybe?

The short answer is that James behaved that way because that's who he is. He wasn't showing off. If he had been, he would have picked a much more complicated subject. Believe it or not, this was his attempt to fit in. And when he observed everyone looking at him *in that way*, he mentally kicked himself, yet again. He started to turn red, but in spite of feeling like an outcast, he figured that if they couldn't appreciate a reference to Greek mythology, it was *their* problem, not his. He wandered off with a battered copy of Ovid's *Metamorphoses* under his arm.

As an adolescent, male bi-nines are notorious for extreme moodiness and for keeping to themselves. Their parents worry as they observe their sons starting to embrace what could be called the darker side of human nature. Their taste in music, literature, and fashion starts to veer toward the experimental and bleak, and parents note a bizarre infatuation with the psychedelic counterculture of the late '60s and '70s. Bi-nine adolescents will delve into the writings of Jack Kerouac, Thomas Pynchon, Hunter S. Thompson, and Joan Didion, as readily as they will listen to *all* the collected works of the Beatles, Rolling Stones, Doors, Grateful Dead, Velvet Underground, and Jefferson Airplane, to name but a few. Incidentally, the more Christian bi-nines have a tendency to memorize the lyrics to *Jesus Christ Superstar* and *Godspell*, much to the chagrin of their secular peers. Particularly enamored with Timothy Leary, Baba Ram Dass, Andy Warhol, the Black Panthers, Ravi Shankar, and, of course, the Woodstock concert, more than a few youthful bi-nines have been known to make "spiritual pilgrimages" to Haight-Ashbury and similar locations.

Unfortunately, this is when relations start souring between bi-nine boys and their parents. Who can blame either party? Dog and cat parents are genuinely perplexed by their bi-nine son's changes during adolescence: His moodiness and general taciturn behavior unsettles them, his virtual obsession with the '60s and '70s strikes them as inappropriate in a child of the '90s. As one exasperated dog mother said to her son, "Why can't you be like your peers, and be into techno, hiphop, and whatever else it is you Generation X kids are supposed to be doing?!"

In any case, when the bi-nine male decides to take a year-long independent study program so he can write his college thesis on the philosophy behind *Zen and the Art of Motorcycle Maintenance*, cat, dog, and even bi-nine parents will put their respective paws down firmly. It should be noted that while many cat, dog, and bi-nine parents were, in fact, very active in the heyday of the '60s, they're no longer into the "tune-in, turn-on, drop-out" scene. (In

undiscovered chamber. When Fox Mulder pleads his case to the deaf ears of his bureau chief is another prime example of how these men will persevere, even in the face of skepticism and ridicule. It's not that they are only idealistic; it's that they're convinced what they believe in is true. Conventional causes don't interest them, but just let them get a whiff of a mystery or be embroiled in a social injustice, and you'll see a fire in their eyes.

When it comes to sex, the bi-nine man is a bit of a late bloomer. His precociousness and sensitivity lead him to a first relationship with an older woman. Take Dustin Hoffman's character in *The Graduate*, for example. After this initiation into the art of love and romance, bi-nine men are usually highly in tune with their partner's sexual and emotional needs. However, we must confess that the bi-nine man can also like experimental sex, even suggesting that you attend special workshops on sexuality. In fact, the bi-nine man may have you attending all sorts of workshops and encounter groups in an effort to help you raise your sexual and spiritual awareness to a level more compatible with his own. One dog woman we interviewed, Arlene, got turned on to yoga by her bi-nine boyfriend and is now a highly respected yoga teacher in Los Angeles.

Relationships with bi-nine men, though often rewarding, are rarely conventional. With their unique minds, dramatic mood swings, predisposition to intensity, and unorthodox behavior, bi-nines are full of surprises. If you're someone who appreciates predictability in people or like those who tread the beaten path, avoid the bi-nine male (or female, for that matter), for he will shake your world without even trying. Conversely, if you're up for a real challenge, the bi-nine man will prove to be endlessly stimulating on every level you can imagine—and on some you can't. Try to figure him out, he dares you!

The Bi-nine Woman

Known as something of a Casanova, Bruce counseled his friend Harry in the art of love: "With dog women, you just never know what they'll say. Remember that, and don't look surprised if in the middle of a cocktail party they loudly announce that you have something green in between your teeth."

Harry nodded intently, making mental notes.

"Cat women…well, you'll never know *what* they're thinking, so if you're dating a cat woman and you think everything is fine—and then suddenly she leaves you—just keep in mind that it's really to be expected and try not to take it personally."

Harry reached for his pen and paper; mental notes weren't enough. These pearls of wisdom clearly needed to be preserved for posterity.

The Bi-nine Personality

Bruce momentarily paused, and then burst into laughter. "And with bi-nine women, you just never know what they'll wear!"

Harry glanced at his notes. They read, "Dog women have no tact, cat women sound dangerous (avoid unless very desirable), and bring some extra clothes if you ever have to introduce a bi-nine woman to Mom, Dad, and Aunt Edna."

Satisfied, Harry folded his notes up and realized that the mysteries of women had finally been demystified for him. Fortified by this knowledge, he strode confidently out the door.

Bruce watched his friend leave but remained deep in thought on the subject of bi-nine women. He had recently introduced his conservative parents to Samantha, and when she strolled into their suburban home with her dyed jet black hair in a chignon, wearing skintight cigarette pants, a form-fitting fuchsia top, and a vintage leopard skin jacket, he could see his mother's eyebrows arch.

Something about Samantha's gazellelike grace compelled Bruce deeply. Ever since their first date, he had had a feeling that Samantha wouldn't necessarily be around for a long time, so he always pretended that each day with her would be his last. He felt silly confiding this fear to his mother, and when she asked Bruce why he was so enamored of Samantha, his answers made absolutely no sense at all. The truth is, Bruce loved Samantha for all those paradoxical reasons that make so many of us either like or love bi-nine women: They are forceful but incredibly vulnerable, ruthless but oddly compassionate, life affirming yet deeply cynical.

"Mom," Bruce suddenly exclaimed in the middle of their conversation, "now I know what it is about Samantha that's so unique. It's like she's two different things at the same time. She's the yin *and* the yang!"

A 100 percent dog personality, his mother was alarmed, and her protection instincts kicked immediately into high gear. Obviously her son was smitten by this Samantha creature, and she didn't want him, the epitome of a dog man, to be devastated by the wiles of this exotic woman. After all, she had her own suspicions about Samantha: The young woman seemed positively schizophrenic.

We must confess that Bruce's mother isn't the first (and certainly won't be the last) to wonder if a bi-nine woman is a little on the schizophrenic side. Let us assure you, bi-nine women, on the whole, don't suffer from a split personality, but they are creatures who thrive on living a life full of contradictions. Bi-nine women usually elicit more than a few raised eyebrows the first time they're seen. **There's an inherent wildness and androgynous appeal present that most people find intriguing, if not intimi-**

The Bi-nine Personality

dating. Explaining why you're attracted to a bi-nine woman is like telling someone why you're fascinated by the women Picasso painted; they contain everything, the earth, moon, sky, and stars, and yet somehow remain absolutely themselves.

Even as a child, the other girls in Samantha's class would stare at her distrustingly, somehow sensing her innate difference. She was pretty but not in an overly feminine or girlish way, intelligent but in an unconventional manner, and even as an eight-year-old, Samantha had an altogether distinct collection of hats. By her junior year in high school, Samantha was branded as a maverick by most of her peers. The young women in her class, in particular, still didn't know what to make of her, and her pattern of being perceived as an outsider continued.

There was the time in the locker room before gym class when everyone saw her first tattoo, a yin and yang symbol, of course, prominently displayed on her left shoulder. And then there was the time she shaved the sides of her head and dyed the remaining mohawk fire-engine red. Finally, let's not forget the skintight black leather pants and camisole she wore on prom night. Her peers were bewildered by her sense of fashion, intimidated by her knowledge, and envious of the way she unselfconsciously mingled with people from all walks of life. And

Like Cats and Dogs

although Samantha never knew it, many of them actually admired her for always having the integrity to be who she was in the face of their censure.

In college, Samantha, like many bi-nine women, came into her own. She was known for her unusually high aptitude in the arts and humanities, specifically in literature, foreign languages, and poetry writing. In the Scrabble competitions held at her college, Samantha easily won every single year. For some reason, many bi-nine women are incredibly adept at crossword puzzles, cryptograms, and word games.

Of course, Samantha was also recognized for her musical talents during college. She lived in Bloomsbury House, well-known for its bohemian attitudes regarding sexuality, as well as for its all-night poetry and music slams. She shopped at flea markets and secondhand stores, which enabled her to perfect the uniquely sensual look that would define her for years to come. And that was just the beginning. She drove an orange 1972 Saab recklessly, playing Janis Joplin, Patti Smith, and Courtney Love (her idol) at full blast. And while the bi-nine men in her life were busy obsessing about '60s and '70s memorabilia and *X-Files* trivia, she was arranging gigs for her all-girls blues band on the local college circuit. Her band, the Sunday School Girls, had gained attention because of her edgy love lyrics and her enticing, raspy, low voice.

The Bi-nine Personality

We would be remiss in our duties if we didn't also broach the all-important question of the bi-nine woman's affinity for exploring other dimensions of reality. Early on, bi-nine women develop an appetite for living life on the edge. **They enjoy pushing themselves to the brink of their physical and psychological limits, even to the point of endangering their lives.** Ever the thrill-seeker, bi-nine women enjoy activities and people that are *intense*. These creatures will dabble in mind-altering drugs and engage in other metaphysical experiences such as transcendental meditation, Zen Buddhism, and Sufi mysticism.

Whether or not they use drugs is hardly the point: **They take the cultivation and growth of the soul as their life's primary motivation.** So, don't be surprised to hear that your best bi-nine girlfriend suddenly decided to cancel her engagement and fly off to India in search of a guru she's been enamored of for years. On the other hand, take it in stride when your bi-nine friend donates the proceeds of her new Internet concept (which eventually nets three million dollars) to an obscure monastery in Tibet. Like we've been saying, *anything* is possible with the bi-nine woman, especially regarding spirituality and altruism.

This brings us to yet another unique feature of the bi-nine woman's personality, her complete disinterest in material things. As we've noted, since this woman operates on a largely spiritual plain, we suggest you brush up

Bi-nine Woman Characteristics

Mysterious	Progressive
Iconoclastic	Sarcastic
Tolerant	Unconventional
Passionate	Androgynous
Expansive	Spiritual

on your philosophy and the premises behind the major world religions before you even attempt to impress her. Have we mentioned that these women are usually Phi Beta Kappa members without even trying? One bi-nine woman we interviewed, Anita, sent back her Phi Beta Kappa key with a brief letter condemning the organization for exclusivity. "But that's the whole point, isn't it?" argued her cat man boyfriend. Anita shrugged her shoulders and, wouldn't you know, was dating a different, in her words "more spiritually evolved," man by the end of the week. Okay, so these lovely creatures can be just a bit judgmental.

But, you're wondering what ever happened with Bruce and Samantha? Although they dated for several more months, Samantha abruptly left for The Netherlands, much to Bruce's mother's relief. Bruce still speaks to her, and thinks about how they first met at a Kurt Cobain memorial. She had been wearing an all-black hemp outfit that day, and Bruce had thought she looked so adorable that he couldn't help flirting with her. Even then, he had known that there was something fleeting about her, almost ephemeral.

In their last conversation, Samantha had confided to him that, after so many years of searching, she had finally located bi-nine heaven: Amsterdam. Bruce smiles when he thinks of Samantha working in a hip, artsy gourmet coffee shop during the day, taking her advanced yoga classes in the morning, and writing poetry at night. He can vividly imagine her working as a part-time DJ at a popular nightclub for bi-nines. Thinking of her sultry dancing makes him deeply nostalgic for a moment, but he realizes some things in life are simply meant to be enjoyed and then let go. Besides, a cute dog woman has just moved into his apartment building. Hmm...who knows?

CASE STUDIES

DEREK
The Story of a Bi-nine Man Living Betwixt and Between

Derek woke up, bathed in sweat. He glanced at his alarm clock, which read 4:20 A.M.; he sighed deeply. Derek had been having the same nightmare for over three months now, sometimes as often as four times a week. It was starting to drive him out of his mind.

In the nightmare, his girlfriend, Joan, was irate, much angrier than he'd ever seen her. She kept pelting him with what looked like hand mirrors, and she would throw one after the other, aiming at his face but saying nothing. He vividly remembered ducking each time she'd sling one at him, and the mirrors would shatter against the wall behind him.

The next stage of the dream became progressively more upsetting. Joan would keep throwing the mirrors and also start screaming at him. He couldn't remember all of it clearly, but it was something like, "Stop lying to me! Who are you, anyway? You're just a chameleon, changing all the time. Just a chameleon...."

Now he was at the worst part of the dream: One of the hand mirrors hit him dead between the eyes, and he fell to the ground in utter agony. Suddenly, he felt the ground under him drag him down; it was like the earth itself was trying to swallow him up. With a start, he realized that he'd been standing on quicksand all along. He would then wake up totally exhausted, feeling suffocated, and gasping for air.

Derek looked at Joan sleeping peacefully in bed beside him. He knew there was a reason he kept having the same dream and felt a fleeting sense of guilt. But why? He had never cheated on Joan, and he couldn't remember ever lying to her about anything important. Overcome with exhaustion, he finally decided to tell Joan about the nightmares the following day.

"Oh, how horrible!" exclaimed Joan sympathetically.

"What do you think it could mean?" asked Derek, curious to hear what her cat woman psychoanalytic personality would come up with.

"Well, it seems a few important images are coming out here. Mirrors symbolize reflection; in this particular context, it seems that I'm trying to force you to face some aspect of yourself. Then I accuse you of being like a chameleon, and I'm upset that you're not one consistent thing. Hmm, that part's really interesting. I guess I've said things to you that were similar to that, haven't I?"

Derek, frowning at the memories, slowly replied, "Yes, you've complained about how you feel insecure with me sometimes, and say my personality changes depending on who I'm with and where I am."

Their conversation was unfortunately cut short because they both had to go to work, but later Derek couldn't help dwelling on Joan's comments. He had an uneasy feeling and confided in his close friend Erin.

"Look, Derek, you know that I've told you this before, but I just don't think you and Joan are compatible. Joan's the kind of cat woman who craves order and simplicity, and you're a bi-nine man who can only thrive with a person who enjoys confusion and ambiguity. And your nightmare just proves it."

Derek looked perplexed.

Erin continued, "You two are like night and day! How can you not see it? Your father is South American, your mother in American, and you were raised on three different continents."

"What does that have to do with anything?" questioned Derek.

"Don't you see?" insisted Erin. "Since you moved around so much as a kid, you *had* to adapt to differing environments. Otherwise, you never would have had friends; you never would have fit in anywhere. This is why Joan thinks of you as a chameleon, because you've been forced to mirror your surroundings to some extent, but what Joan doesn't appreciate is that this is an important part of your personality. It's a vital part of who you are, Derek, and it's not fair for her to demand that you put your personality in some kind of straitjacket for her!"

"No," argued Derek, "it's not that she wants me to really change my identity. It's just that...I don't know."

"Remember how she kept wanting you not to study anthropology?"

"Yeah, that's true," admitted Derek. "She said that she would worry that I'd go into a foreign environment and 'go native.' I didn't take what she said seriously at the time, but I guess there's a pattern here."

"Derek," said Erin slowly, "I want to ask you something. Joan's lived in one state all her life, while you moved six times by the time you were thirteen. All of Joan's friends are similar to her, and everyone knows your friends are so incompatible that it's impossible for them to be civil to one another if they're in one room together. Since you're obviously so radically different, what exactly is her attraction for you?"

Derek knew the answer but didn't feel like getting into it. He loved Joan precisely because she was his polar opposite. He loved her stability, for instance, and the fact that she had grown up in one house for the first eighteen years of her life. He loved how her family was the ideal nuclear family—with parents who weren't divorced, two kids (a boy and a girl, of course), and a dog. By contrast, his own parents divorced when he was five, he was an only child, and he had moved so much in his life (because his father was a diplomat) that he never knew how to respond when someone asked him where his home was. The truth was, he never felt like he had one.

After hugging Erin good-bye, Derek felt that he had gained some perspective on his nightmare. He felt it was a way for his psyche to tell him that Joan had been pressuring him, more than he'd realized, to conform to her lifestyle. If the mirror did symbolize reflection, then Joan was clearly trying to impose some kind of reflection on him that wasn't his own. No wonder he had been feeling so suffocated! Suddenly it came to him, the one mirror that hit him hard represented something tangible in their relationship, and he knew what it was: It represented their continual argument about whether he should study anthropology or not. Over dinner, he broached the subject again.

"Joan, I've decided it's best if I pursue anthropology," Derek stated.

"Not again," Joan said with some annoyance. "I thought we'd already discussed this!"

"Maybe we did, but I guess I'm not really satisfied with the decision that you—I mean we..."

But it was too late. They both knew what Derek meant.

"Look, I'm sorry," Joan said. "I didn't think I was pushing you to do something you didn't want to do. It's just that you've already traveled so extensively in your life, and I thought you wanted more consistency now."

Derek replied, "I'm not blaming you. You're right, I think a part of me craves being one stable thing—kind of like you—and I've told you before that my life has often felt so fragmented and confusing to me."

"So why go into a field that mimics the craziness of your childhood? That's what I don't understand. You're attracted to a career that will never give you the kind of base that you want. You'll always be traveling to foreign countries, doing fieldwork."

"I think what I'm realizing is that this gray, ambiguous space in my life is actually something I'm comfortable with. It's simply who I am."

Joan nodded and said nothing. They both sensed their relationship was in trouble. They had reached a stalemate.

They continued dating casually for the next few weeks, but as Derek became more and more assertive, Joan became increasingly frustrated. Finally, the tension was so palpable that they separated. During their separation, Joan became established as a magazine writer and, in the midst of writing an article on multiculturalism, had an epiphany: Part of the reason Derek had compelled her so deeply was because of his multiethnic background and because he had been so refreshingly different from so many people around her. Now she felt silly to have ever felt threatened by the very part of him that had attracted her in the first place.

Derek, for his part, dated casually after they broke up, but while he was sometimes more compatible with other women, his heart wasn't really in it. Finally deciding that he was destined to be a perpetual bachelor, he flew off to Brazil to do fieldwork. After a few months, he was surprised to get a letter from Joan saying that she'd love to see him again, and was hoping to visit him. Ecstatic, Derek invited her to stay with him, and within two weeks he was picking Joan up at the airport in Rio de Janeiro.

Realizing that they both had a sincere desire to make their relationship work, Joan decided to stay on in Rio for a few months with Derek. Affirming their love for each other, Joan confessed that she loved Derek for his difference, and he, in turn, admitted that though he loved anthropology, his priority was building a home with Joan. They settled on a compromise: After every three years in the United States, Derek would spend six months doing fieldwork in South America, and Joan would accompany him while writing freelance articles. The rest of the time they would reside in a wonderful apartment in the heart of San Francisco.

"How perfect it all is," Derek mused, "and how ironic that the nightmare that had haunted me for months has ultimately enabled me to heal."

CHRIS

The Saga of a Bi-nine Married to a Cat but Cheating with a Dog!

Have you ever been deeply dissatisfied with the present state of your life? Have you ever felt that you have been living a lie all along and then decided that, finally, the time has come to live your life *on your terms*, regardless of the price? It happened to Chris, and this is her story.

The Bi-nine Personality

Things somehow just weren't adding up for Chris. She had vague feelings of discontent but wasn't able to identify the source. Some days she yearned for the neat, orderly life she shared with Charles; other days she found refuge in Michael's passionate and unpredictable world. Sexually, she couldn't make up her mind either. The sex she and Charles had, although not as rough or spontaneous as that with Michael, had a quality of finesse and precision that she began to miss. Charles with his svelte body and cool, precise hands gave one side of her personality a form of satisfaction it craved. By contrast, Michael's spontaneity and experimental nature unleashed her hidden passion. Yearning for both men in different ways, she was tortured by their demand for her to choose one over the other.

What had happened to bring Chris to this breaking point, you ask? Good question. Probably the biggest impact on Chris had happened earlier, when Kat, her mother, appalled by her desire to become an actress, persuaded Chris to marry Charles, an upstanding cat man real estate agent from her uncle's real estate firm, "for her own good."

After two years of a sedentary and safe life, something simply snapped. Seeing an audition for an off-off Broadway play, Chris decided to give it a try. Michael, the director, was a charming dog personality who was so impressed with her that she got the leading role. Needless to say, taking the role wreaked havoc in her life. Charles, for instance, cattily commented that she was being irrational since ultimate success would never come to her through the theater, while her father, in his usual catatonic fashion, refused to discuss the matter.

In standing up to Charles and her parents, Chris remembered what an outsider she sometimes felt like in her family, with their strict adherence to all the classic cat values of order, tidiness, and caution. Thinking back, she realized she had never been affirmed for expressing the full complexity of her feelings. There was the time when she was eight, for example, and had painted her closet doors with neon green and magenta Magic Markers. Her mother, unwilling to accept her explanations, lectured her extensively on the evils of an aesthetically undisciplined life.

How about the time when she was fifteen and dyed her hair violet as a personal statement? Her mother simply wouldn't hear about her friends, her music, or the "in" look. Instead, Chris was immediately dragged to a salon in a disastrous attempt to make her hair look "respectable." Reflecting on all of this, Chris realized she had felt pulled in opposite directions throughout her life. Although she had been taught to respect order, a part of her seemed to crave chaos.

Not long after her decision to remain in the play, Chris and Michael began spending long evenings after rehearsals talking about theater and the arts. He was an intense, impulsive, social, and charismatic man who had never been married but who sustained a string of serially monogamous relationships with his leading ladies. He would write, drink, and socialize late into the night, waking up in the middle of the day to an apartment that smelled of cigarettes and wine. Unlike Chris's family, Michael affirmed her writing and acting, encouraging the creative and spontaneous side of her personality to emerge. During rehearsals, he pushed her to her emotional limits, and then, one evening after a particularly ugly fight with Charles, Chris found herself at Michael's apartment—and soon after—in his bed. Her first affair had begun, and with a dog man at that.

Finally, after a year of vacillations, indecisions, and utter agony, Chris decided to leave both her husband and Michael to take an apartment by herself in the city. Although she still loved Charles and cared for Michael, she knew that one of them alone would be fundamentally unable to satisfy all her needs. Most important, she understood that her life before the theater—although never explicitly bad—would never, ever be enough for her again.

Chris now lives a rather bohemian existence in Sante Fe with her cat, LuLu, and her dalmatian, Pongo. She has many bi-nine friends, several lovers, and sports a distinctive tattoo of an Egyptian ankh above her pierced navel.

CHAPTER 4

Famous Dog, Cat, and Bi-nine People

Hollywood Celebrities

Dogs	Cats
Katharine Hepburn	Audrey Hepburn
Harrison Ford	Eddie Murphy
Sandra Bullock	Halle Berry
Jack Nicholson	Will Smith
Michael Douglas	Jim Carrey
Kevin Costner	Michelle Pfeiffer
Claudia Schiffer	Christy Turlington
Alicia Siverstone	Liv Tyler

Famous Dog, Cat, and Bi-nine People

Dogs (cont.)   Cats (cont.)

Dogs (cont.)	Cats (cont.)
Robert Redford	Meryl Streep
Denzel Washington	Angela Bassett
Helena Christiansen	Naomi Campbell
Clint Eastwood	Tony Randall
Whoopi Goldberg	Jodie Foster
Tom Hanks	James Spader
Howard Stern	Vanessa Williams
Robin Williams	Billy Crystal
Jane Fonda	Sharon Stone (frequently mistaken for a bi-nine)

Bi-nines

Kurt Cobain	Courtney Love
Madonna	Dennis Rodman
Oscar Wilde	Virginia Woolf
Divine	RuPaul
James Dean	River Phoenix
Sigourney Weaver	Michael Jackson
Sandra Bernhardt	Marlon Brando

Like Cats and Dogs

TV Personalities

Dogs	Cats
Oscar Madison, Jack Klugman	Felix Ungar, Tony Randall
Sam Malone, Ted Danson	Diane Chambers, Shelley Long
Kramer, Michael Richards	Seinfeld, Jerry Seinfeld
Laverne, Penny Marshall	Shirley, Cindy Williams
Richie Cunningham, Ron Howard	The Fonz, Henry Winkler
Doug Ross, George Clooney	Dylan McKay, Luke Perry
Murphy Brown, Candice Bergen	Miles Silverberg, Grant Shaud
Billy Campbell, Andrew Shue	Amanda Woodward, Heather Locklear
Superman, Dean Cain	Lois Lane, Teri Hatcher
Kathie Lee Gifford	Regis Philbin
Oprah	Montel Williams
Barbara Walters	Diane Sawyer
Tom Brokaw	Dan Rather
Katie Couric	Ann Curry
Al Roker	Matt Lauer
David Letterman	Conan O'Brien
Paul Reiser	Michael J. Fox
Helen Hunt	Drew Carey

Famous Dog, Cat, and Bi-nine People

Bi-nines

Fox Mulder,
David Duchovny

Mr. Spock,
Leonard Nimoy

TV Shows

Dog People Watch	Cat People Watch
Friends	*Friends*
ER	*Frasier*
Mad About You	*Seinfeld*
Party of Five	*Melrose Place*
Hercules: Legendary Journeys	*Xena, Warrior Princess*
The Rosie O'Donnell Show	*Leeza*
Cops	*House of Style*
All My Children	*One Life to Live*
FOX News	*ABC World News Tonight*
The Simpsons	*Beverly Hills 90210*

Bi-nines Watch

X-Files

Sliders

Unsolved Mysteries

Star Trek: The Next Generation

The Robin Byrd Show
(and we know quite a few cats and dogs tuning in as well!)

Like Cats and Dogs

Celebrity Couples

Famous Dog Couples

Kim Basinger	Alec Baldwin
Susan Sarandon	Tim Robbins
Goldie Hawn	Kurt Russell
Maria Shriver	Arnold Schwarzenegger
Meg Ryan	Dennis Quaid
Joanne Woodward	Paul Newman
Mary Matalin	James Carville
Jane Fonda	Ted Turner

Famous Cat Couples

Kate Moss	Johnny Depp
Whitney Houston	Bobby Brown

Famous Bi-nine Couples

David Bowie	Iman
Laurence Olivier	Vivian Leigh
Sam Shephard	Jessica Lange

Famous Dog, Cat, and Bi-nine People

Famous Interspeciel Couples

Dogs	Cats
Tom Cruise	Nicole Kidman
John F. Kennedy, Jr.	Carolyn Bassette Kennedy
Warren Beatty	Annette Bening
Demi Moore	Bruce Willis
Kyra Sedgwick	Kevin Bacon
Ellen DeGeneres	Anne Heche
Maury Povich	Connie Chung
Bill Clinton	Hillary Rodham Clinton
Melissa Etheridge	Julie Cypher
Tipper Gore	Al Gore

...and the ones that didn't last (rumor has it, they fought like cats and dogs)

Dogs	Cats
Roseanne Barr	Tom Arnold
Mia Farrow	Woody Allen
Princess Diana	Prince Charles
Julia Roberts	Lyle Lovett
Winona Ryder	Johnny Depp
Donald Trump	Marla Maples

Like Cats and Dogs

Dogs (cont.)	Cats (cont.)
Richard Gere	Cindy Crawford
Sonny	Cher
Ed Burns	Maxine Bahns
Al Pacino	Diane Keaton
Brad Pitt	Gwyneth Paltrow

Fashion

Dogs	Cats
Ralph Lauren	Halston
Karl Lagerfeld	Isaac Mizrahi
Tommy Hilfiger	Giorgio Armani
Donnatella and Gianni Versace	Calvin Klein
Gucci	Prada
Anna Sui	Donna Karan
Helmut Lang	Jil Sander

Bi-nines

The Gap

J. Crew

cK

CHAPTER 5

Astrology and the Cat, Dog, and Bi-nine Personality

Aries Cat Person

You've been staring at a very attractive man at your best friend's party for some time now. In trying to determine whether or not he's a cat or dog personality, you note that he seems simultaneously aggressive and reserved. You're aware that the typical cat man appears aloof, subtly extracting more information than he gives. In this instance, however, you just don't know how to interpret this man's vital presence or his seeming nonchalance. As he walks over to you, your brows furrow; you feel under pressure to say the right thing. Certain that his strategic air makes him a cat, you quickly try to determine what kind. As he extends his hand, something clicks, and in your not-so-subtle way assert, "Aries, an Aries cat man, right?" He's slightly disconcerted, obviously unaccustomed to being beaten to the punch line of a person's character. But he smiles and quickly recovers his poise. Now it's his turn. Looking you dead in the eyes, he says, "And you, I presume, are a Sagittarius dog woman."

Your typical Aries cat person is aggressive, self-assured, and direct. Unlike his or her cat counterparts, the Aries cat is much less concerned with others' opinions. In fact, these individuals are self-focused and tend to disregard what other people think or say about them. They consider the world simply a medium through which they can carry out their unique plan of action, and *action* is a key word with the cat Aries. They are highly motivated workers with no patience for those who don't share their drive to succeed.

Seldom afflicted with depression or pessimism, the Aries cat person seizes every opportunity life presents with gusto. A prime example is our Aries cat man who managed not only to recover from our Sagittarius dog woman's offensive but to reposition himself as an active player. Remember, these cats will land on their feet no matter what. And you might want to bear this in mind when it comes to affairs of the heart. Your typical Aries feline will overwhelm you with the force of their seduction. They may pursue you for months, follow you across the globe, or send you ten dozen roses. Whatever their tack, it will be sure to dizzy your senses. (Unless you're a Scorpio cat, that is. For some reason Aries and Scorpio cats mix like oil and water.)

Once you're firmly entrenched under the Aries spell, you will find yourself involved with a deeply sensual person. Aries cat people love romance and sensuality. Surely the best way to hold their attention is to buy a book like the *Kama Sutra* so you can brush up on your erotic repertoire. Don't forget that Aries cat lovers cannot bear to be bored by their intimate other. They invest a great deal of time and effort in dreaming up new ways to keep the fire of passion burning, and they expect you to behave similarly. So, ditch those flannel pajamas and old T-shirts and try something in silk or, if you're feeling especially provocative, sleep with nothing on at all except a dash of perfume or cologne!

Aries Dog Person

Find the leader of a group, the most outspoken person in a crowd or the person making the most changes in an organization, and you've probably got yourself an Aries dog person. These people are assertive pioneers who believe all boundaries will yield to their will, and they're usually right. Scoffing at the limits that intimidate others, they scream *carpe diem* while pursuing their goals with unquenchable enthusiasm. Naturally, this means they have no qualms about demanding of others what they demand of themselves. Don't be surprised, for instance, if your Aries dog boss calls you at three in the morning to discuss currency fluctuations in Tokyo. As a rule, these people sleep less than average and attempt to do twice as much in their day than most people. With their keen sense perceptions and razor sharp intelligence, they thrive on always being on the move.

It is important to note that although the average Aries dog person likes money, and usually makes quite a bit of it, financial success is not the only motivation. In fact, this person usually achieves success and makes money as a consequence of doing enjoyable work. Because of their iron will and astounding power of perseverance, Aries dog people can attribute their success not to greed, as others might think, but to their knack for sticking valiantly through the hard times and waiting for the better times. It's not even that they're especially patient; it's just that they can't imagine not succeeding in something they've put their minds to. To be honest, you could almost say conceit is their secret weapon.

Astrology

When it comes to romance, the Aries dog is a bit less flirtatious and philandering than the usual dog personality. In other words, this individual genuinely tries to be the soul of fidelity. If an Aries dog man sets his sights on a woman, she can believe that she's his one and only because he understands commitment and knows how to make it fun. Willing to spend a lifetime looking for the hero or heroine to fulfill their romantic dreams, Aries dog men want to be your knight in shining armor, while Aries dog women are the embodiment of the ideal '90s woman—intelligent, sensual, and independent.

However, there's a slight catch. These people have a propensity for irrational and extreme jealousy. You see, once the Aries dog has made a commitment, he or she will honor it heart and soul. Naturally, the Aries dog will expect a partner to do the same with equal sincerity and ardor. Therefore, even a lingering look at your physical trainer or an extra session with your attractive squash partner could set off a jealousy alert button. We recommend anticipating an Aries dog's suspicions and mitigating them as soon as possible. If all else fails, say in an articulate and firm manner that such behavior is irrational. Keep in mind that the Aries dog person can bounce back from a lot, but betrayal is unforgivable. The last thing these canines want to do is endanger what they feel has been hard-won trust, and rightly so. In violating their faith in the integrity of your relationship, the Aries dog will leave you with dizzying speed. And you may not realize it immediately, but losing an Aries dog man or woman will surely be an irreplaceable loss.

Aries Bi-nine Person

There once was a movie star who literally oozed sensuality, whose temper was legendary, and whose will was law on the set. That actor was Marlon Brando, a classic Aries bi-nine. The Aries bi-nine has a distinct predilection for the limelight. In fact, their intelligence, creativity, and drive merge to create individuals whose very popularity is focused around the mystique of their ego and desires. In short, these people have a way of looming larger than life. Both Marlon Brando and Bette Davis were more than mere movie stars; they were cinematic power brokers whose charisma on and off screen preserves them as idols forever.

Notice how little physical perfection matters when it comes to the powerful sexual allure that Aries bi-nines exude. Betty Davis was far from being considered physically perfect, yet her sultry style, smoky voice, and self-indulgent attitude did more to charm everyone around her than all the physical perfection in the world. With Brando and Davis, as with most Aries bi-nines, the allure lies precisely in their less-than-attractive features. Their explosive rages, piercing brilliance, and ruthless ambition are evidence of their dark side, which helps to spin a web of charismatic fascination.

What the Aries bi-nine abhors most is a lack of individuality. Using every tool at their disposal to get attention and separate themselves from the masses, these people refuse to blend into the background. Unequivocal mastery of a subject, field, skill, or sport is one tool these individuals will use to distinguish themselves. Vincent van Gogh, for instance, spent years slavishly learning to draw and paint, only to reinvent the very rules through which we understand art.

This brings us to yet another important key to the bi-nine personality; being prolific is secondary to improving the established rules. In this way, like the dog and cat Aries, they are pioneers, entrepreneurials who know no limits. We recently interviewed a physician from Doctors Without Borders, a team of physicians who offer their services to the front-line of war-torn countries, and we weren't surprised to discover she was an Aries bi-nine who felt stagnated by the predictability of a simple practice in Chicago. What was her specialty, you ask? Brain surgery.

Like Cats and Dogs

Taurus Cat Person

A feline of few words, the Taurus cat is frequently described as "the strong and silent type." This individual is usually courageous and relatively undaunted in the face of life's difficulties. In fact, the Taurus cats usually succeed in everything they undertake because they are better able to ride out the turbulent spots than, say, their Gemini or Pisces cousins. Consider Dawn. During our interview she told us how she had started her own business, gone bankrupt, and seen her childhood home burn down. In the midst of her shock and sorrow, she had taken her LSATs and applied to law school. She presently works as a highly successful lawyer in Chicago. Now that's Taurus cat staying power for you; these felines aren't only aloof, they can be downright unflinching once they decide to achieve something.

Although some people have complained that these Taureans "behave like androids who are devoid of feelings," we believe this is a misconception. The truth is that Taurus cat people embody the saying, Still waters run deep. Incredibly sensitive and supportive of those they care for, these individuals will tactfully give full and unequivocal support to you in public, while reserving any criticisms of your behavior for a gentle discussion at home. After all, they are fundamentally pragmatists, and rather than dreaming of how things could be, they are content to work with things the way they are. Incidentally, keep in mind that the Taurus cat person needs to protect your—and their—privacy, a nonnegotiable point that has caused serious rifts with those from the more public signs such as Leo, Sagittarius, and Gemini.

Enamored of beauty and grace, these people will surround themselves with rare and precious, or just subtle and harmonious, pieces of art. Taurus cat people have been known to own opulent mansions, while the modest ones opt for simple elegance. In an effort to find an outlet for their aesthetic interests, these individuals gravitate to careers in art collecting, antiques selling, or opera singing. Tracy, whom we interviewed, told us she started out as a representative for a pharmaceuticals company, but after a career change, now happily works for Sotheby's.

When it comes to love, this individual is nothing if not self-controlled and disciplined. Before you ever see a glimmer of Taurus feline passion, you will have been carefully watched handling a number of different situations, from buying groceries to hanging out with friends to entertaining business clients. You should be aware that while the Taurus cat man or woman may appreciate your attractiveness, it won't mean much if you're not also reliable, trustworthy, and grounded in reality. Like their Taurus counterparts, these cats are some of the most down-to-earth folks you'll ever meet. Remember, it's not that they don't like the more volatile signs, it's simply that when it comes to settling down, they know the difference between a sexual fling and the real thing. In short, they value someone who, like themselves, will put money in the bank and be committed to working on problems with maturity, rather than just walking out.

Taurus Dog Person

Friendly, loyal, and not taken in by glamorous superficiality, a Taurus canine's feet are firmly planted on the ground. While not the most extroverted of all the signs, he or she is certainly the most reliable. It is true that this individual mulls things over meticulously, ignoring comments about being a "stick in the mud." Cautious to a fault, the Taurus dog person will rarely leap before looking carefully. In other words, don't expect to find a Taurus man or woman at an elopement chapel in Vegas. Also, should you have something to hide, like a gambling habit or an unsavory past, be sure that you allow your Taurus lover enough time to adjust to the confession. Don't worry, these canines won't be judgmental as long as you're honest with them about your past; otherwise they'll never trust you.

Astrology

But let's not get so mired in their sedentary qualities before we explore the unique things these people have to offer. First of all, they are die-hard romantics who believe in candlelight dinners and honeymoons in Venice, especially a gentle glide down those mystical canals at dusk. Taurus dog women, known for their shapely bodies, have a reputation for being intelligent and for their refreshingly matter-of-fact attitude toward sex and relationships. Taurus dog men are usually athletic and forceful with an intensity that attracts the notice of powerful people around them. Orson Welles in his success is a classic example of a Taurean dog person.

Talented at acquiring, investing, and increasing capital, Taureans are known for their financial acumen, and the Taurean dog is no exception. Whether it's saving quarters in their ceramic piggy bank as a child or managing hundreds of millions of dollars as an investment banker, Taurus canines have a knack for saving and making money. Although this particular canine can be unbearably stubborn, even succumbing to moments of pure greed, it is usually possible to temper these less desirable qualities through your own model of generosity and graciousness.

Consider Jerome, whose family was plummeted into poverty by the closing of the steel mills in Pittsburgh. By shining shoes, cleaning yards, and working nights as a janitor, he managed to save enough money to move to New

Like Cats and Dogs

York where he worked as a custodian by day, and took correspondence courses in the evening. By thirty-two he had saved enough, and learned enough, to buy his first building. In the next several years, Jerome bought five more buildings, three of which happened to be located in the heart of an up-and-coming neighborhood in Brooklyn. In the meantime, he helped put his siblings through school, bought his parents a home, and earned a master's degree in business. Now affluent and well educated, he is engaged to an intelligent and motivated woman from his hometown. Once again, this is a testimony to the Taurus dog person's drive and endurance. If what you desire is a stable home, solid mutual fund investments, and a college savings plan for the kids, the Taurus dog person is the one you've been waiting for.

Taurus Bi-nine Person

During a casting call for an independent film, there sat a group of fifteen young women, the majority of whom were dressed to kill in tight bell bottoms, cropped shirts, and trendy piercings. But one woman with large expressive eyes seemed impervious to the fashion trends of the day. Wearing a black cashmere sweater and a pair of perfectly creased and impeccably fitted olive wool trousers, she had pulled her hair back in a twist and secured it with one lacquer red chopstick. Although lean and small boned, she conveyed strength rather than frailty, and her clothes, instead of seeming conservative next to her hip peers, seemed timeless and elegant.

As each woman before her read, the director would cluck in seeming approval as they wept, railed, or otherwise exaggerated their meager lines. When it was her turn, she stood up and—having memorized the lines—looked fearlessly into the director's eyes. Almost whispering her seven sentences with a quiet ferocity that rendered the room completely silent, she put down her script and left, without so much as a backward glance. As legend goes, the director was heard to say, "Now that's star quality." As you'd expect, the director offered her the part that very afternoon, and within two years she was the hottest young actress in independent films. Within three more years, she was considered the most talented and versatile actress in Hollywood, yet, interestingly enough, her style never changed much; her look was always characterized by simplicity, elegance, and unwavering grace.

Although the Taurus bi-nine may appear slightly less dynamic than the Gemini or Leo bi-nine, one should not underestimate the force behind that deceptively placid exterior. This individual is unusually gifted with a subtly magnetic personality. Without appearing to do a thing, these Taureans inexplicably draw others into their circle. The truth is that while the placid Taurus nature can be internal, it is certainly not antisocial. These bi-nines enjoy being surrounded by friends and family and usually travel in an entourage of loved ones. Their home tends to be a vibrant location where everyone who wanders in is always welcome to stay, provided they exude positive energy and loyalty.

You should be aware that since Taurus bi-nines are so talented, they refuse to throw their pearls before swine. In addition, don't expect them to be concerned about proving themselves. They know they're "special" and are completely secure in this knowledge. Once you realize this, they wager a sure bet you'll want to stick around.

Often involved in creative endeavors from writing to making pottery, many Taurus bi-nines love to create things with their own bodies and minds. In fact, it's probably no coincidence that Taurean parents frequently choose to have more than two children. They are attracted to those who recognize, appreciate, and validate their efforts. You can be certain that if you affirm your Taurus bi-nine, the sky is the limit as far as their return of your appreciation. Let's just say that they may buy you a new car, surprise you with a trip to Europe, or compose the most beautiful wedding vows you've ever heard as your wedding gift.

Astrology

Gemini Cat Person

Unpredictable and *inscrutable* are the words most often associated with Gemini cat people. Experts at masking their dual personality, they never let you know what they're really thinking or feeling. [These people wrote the book on not being known.] For them, the powers of the twins are harnessed in the service of keeping the rest of the world guessing. One day your Gemini cat may seem serene and loving, the next volatile and ferocious. Although both extremes represent different aspects of their nature, their strategy causes you to run around in circles, trying to uncover the "real" them. Who knows? Maybe they just feel safer with you chasing your own tail. Certainly, something about the Gemini cat loves to remain shrouded in mystery.

But don't get discouraged, just because these cats won't self-disclose doesn't mean they aren't the epitome of charm, grace, and savoir faire. More than a few politicians are born under the sign of cat Gemini, and, need we tell you, they are extremely effective at marshaling resources, implementing their agendas, and subtly controlling the public. It might behoove you to be careful with these elegant and interesting charmers, or, before you know it, you might find yourself engaged or otherwise helplessly wrapped up in their seductive spell. And if you haven't realized it, they have quite a few personas to seduce you with.

Remember one thing about Gemini cat people: They will go to great lengths to avoid work that is in any way redundant. The reason perhaps is because there are already two of them in there—the Gemini twins, that is. One Gemini feline we interviewed was so frustrated working as a corporate lawyer that he switched to international network news. He now happily reports that every day he gets to participate in a dynamic and ongoing adventure somewhere in the world. Unable to thrive unless they openly express their contradictory nature, these people will often moonlight in the theater, or as artists, poets, writers, or musicians.

The wonderful thing about Gemini cat people is that they can, better than almost all others, understand and embrace the paradoxical and transitory nature of existence. So, if you wake up indecisive—torn between wanting to quit your job and run off to South America or sticking it out in the hope of one day ruling the corporate roost—your Gemini cat lover won't be appalled by your erratic vacillations. (And don't worry, they won't encourage you to discuss Prozac with your therapist either.) They'll just smile knowingly and say something like, "Yeah, life sure is a roller coaster." The pithy remark may not alleviate all your anxieties, but it sure can be comforting to be with someone who isn't threatened by your complexity, isn't it?

Gemini Dog Person

The Gemini dog person has the most visibly dual character of the Gemini lot. Take, for instance, a woman we interviewed from Washington, D.C., whose husband, a Gemini dog, traveled between D.C. and Los Angeles every month. After several years, she discovered that he had a steady girlfriend, as well as a newborn daughter, in Los Angeles. She was flabbergasted; even in the face of incontrovertible proof, she still couldn't believe it. When she confronted her husband, imploring him to explain why he did this when they seemed to have such a vibrant relationship, he replied with a straight face, "But you and Cindy are so different—I love you both. It's just that I feel like a different person with each of you."

Geminis tell us this is a slightly unfortunate aspect of the Gemini dog personality, and that in his own way he probably does love her. However, having reached the end of her otherwise stable Cancer cat rope, she divorced "that schizophrenic, good-for-nothing." Now she's slowly getting her romantic feet wet again with a nice reliable Taurus dog man. Her ex-husband, on the other hand, never fully understood why she doubted his love and still wonders why so many non-Geminis find monogamy appealing.

The dog Gemini, not unlike the cat or bi-nine Gemini, manifests the twin sign most overtly in the form of indecision and restlessness. On Monday, he will be convinced that the living room should be painted dusty blue, and you may find yourself agreeing with his impassioned reasoning for doing so. On Tuesday, you remark how right he was to choose this particular shade of blue and are surprised by his discontented expression as he stares at the freshly painted walls. On Wednesday, just as you're getting used to what the living room looks like, he suddenly decides that the blue is passé and has lined the halls with cans of maize-yellow paint. Wondering if this kaleidoscopic paint display will ever cease, you stifle an urge to scream.

Given this story, it should come as no surprise that these individuals have a tendency not only to sport different personas weekly, but to dress in unpredictable styles—one day as a corporate executive, the next looking like some ultrahip throwback to the '70s, the third in hiphop gear. The fact is that since the Gemini dog doesn't particularly value consistency, they wholeheartedly express the whims of their hopelessly divided selves in creative and interesting ways.

Naturally, this has been known to give a few girl-friends and boyfriends an uneasy feeling about the future. But, don't worry, as the adage goes, If you love something, set it free. In this case, if you love a Gemini dog person, give him or her the freedom to roam, which just might increase the chances of a return visit. And so it goes with the canine twins. But as anyone who's ever felt the confines of unhealthy dependence in love will tell you, at least a Gemini dog person will stay with you for no reason other than sincere affection.

Gemini Bi-nine Person

The mother of a Gemini bi-nine may suspect her lovely little toddler has attention deficit disorder because the child is perpetually on the move. Even at age three they are captivated by everything and everyone around them, trying to move rapidly so they can better take the world in. Full of charisma and unquenchable curiosity, these double twins (bi-nine and Gemini) can't help but be diverted by all that comes their way. We know one Gemini bi-nine who is simultaneously earning a medical degree and a law degree, and all she talks about is how she'll get a doctorate in biochemistry once medical and law school are finished.

Like Cats and Dogs

It's hard to believe, but she's at the top of both her classes and is one of the most attractive and vivacious women on campus with a full social calendar every weekend. As we mere mortals ask how she manages to date, socialize, and study for both course loads without burning out, she looks blasé and responds, "Hmm, you know, I just hate only doing one thing—it's sooo boring!" Unsatisfied by her answer, her friends secretly speculate that there's a Siamese twin trapped inside her doing half the work. But that's the key, isn't it? The Gemini bi-nine has quadruple the energy, intelligence, curiosity, and motivation— they're really four people rolled into one.

Glib, fond of debate, and highly verbal, the Gemini bi-nine has been known to have strong powers of persuasion. Usually this talent won't be wasted on selling used cars, instead try looking up authors from a couple of best-selling self-help books. Whether it's leading workshops on self-esteem or founding a New Age religion, it shouldn't surprise you that this articulate and charismatic leader is a bi-nine born in June.

When it comes to romance, the Gemini bi-nine disdains those who are incapable of adapting. If you seek stability and security, the Gemini bi-nine will definitely not be your cup of tea. Unfortunately, because this bi-nine could be feeling very domestic for the entirety of your courtship, you might not realize the honeymoon is over until it's literally too late. By the time his or her other personality emerges, you may be so invested in the marriage that you're forced to play out a war of attrition in which you relentlessly complain, "But you weren't like this in the beginning!" Usually this assertion gets a withering look from the Gemini bi-nine who can't imagine why anyone would count that as a fault. We suggest topping his or her changeability by trying some latent unpredictability of your own. You could not only realize some new things about yourself, but you might also discover that your Gemini bi-nine has come to see you as a kindred spirit.

Cancer Cat Person

Never lose sight of the fact that the Cancer cat person lives under a shell. In other words, although these people may appear to be accessible, nothing could be further from the truth. You may see one decked out in a beautifully tailored Armani suit, but just scratch beneath the surface, and you'll find a reserved character.

A complex creature, the Cancer cat person can be extroverted one day, yet completely withdrawn and sullen the next. These felines also tend to be a highly cautious lot; don't expect them to give you a loan without interest or to make an investment without first carefully scrutinizing the market.

Like Cats and Dogs

However, it is interesting to notice how wildly their fiscal conservatism is at odds with their desire for affirmation and love. The Cancer cat woman, for example, may gaze at you one morning with her beautifully chiseled face and then coolly inform you that she does not feel appreciated. She will then proceed to curl back up into a ball and pout in solitude for the rest of the day. You, on the other hand, will be completely perplexed since, after all, she isn't exactly the most forthcoming and effusive person you've ever met. But that's just the point: It doesn't matter how defensive, withdrawn, or downright crabby your Cancer cat woman is, she will still expect you to see the real her, showering her with love and attention. Needless to say, life with these creatures can be trying.

During an interview, we were told the story of a darling five-year-old Aries dog child, Suzy, who told her Scorpio cat mother one bright, sunny Saturday that her aunt Carolyn, a Cancer cat woman, was "a selfish." Her mother laughed and said, "You mean 'selfish,' sweetheart, not 'a selfish.'" She then called her sister, Carolyn, and told her the amusing anecdote. "You see, Carolyn," she gloated, "even little Suzy sees your selfish streak, like when you wouldn't let me borrow your cashmere coat last week." Naturally, this sent Carolyn sulking, and when she finally reappeared at a family dinner two weeks later, she was far from her usual buoyant self.

Astrology

Immediately noticing the difference, Suzy demanded that her aunt tell what was wrong. Carolyn looked at the girl, sighed, and blurted out, "Suzy, we do so many fun things together, why do you think I'm selfish?" Everyone looked at Suzy expectantly. Frowning and thinking hard, she momentarily brightened and ran out of the room. Within seconds, she returned holding up a drawing. "Look Aunt Carolyn," she exclaimed. "I made a picture of your 'selfish.'" What Suzy had in her hand was a drawing of a big crab. Suddenly everyone burst into laughter, and Carolyn exclaimed, "Oh, you mean *shellfish*!" Suzy's mother, laughing hardest of all, gasped, "You are a selfish shellfish!" Carolyn turned red and stood up indignantly, saying, "You probably knew what Suzy meant all along, and this is your way of picking on me just like when we were kids," and stormed out of the house.

Needless to say, Carolyn did eventually forgive her sister but not without several weeks of giving her the cold shoulder. (Consider this a testimony as to how long the Cancer cat individual can hold a grudge.) It might be worth adding that Carolyn was never really upset with Suzy; the cat crab has a very strong protective streak when it comes to those younger or weaker than themselves. As for their selfishness, let's just say that perhaps the best method to adopt with them is Ben Franklin's motto, Never a borrower nor a lender be.

Cancer Dog Person

Your Cancer dog person is nothing if not a deeply feeling and sensitive individual. What these people feel and what they think are so closely connected that they can't tell them apart, so it's best to get used to it from the beginning. Don't be surprised, for example, when your Cancer dog partner turns to you in the midst of an argument over whether you were rude to the dinner guests and says with exasperation, "I think you felt annoyed, and Jean must have thought so too." The classic Cancer dog line is, "I think I felt" or "I think you felt."

Sensitivity is probably what makes this sign one of the most nurturing you will encounter. Unlike the Cancer cat person, this canine's tough outer shell is just for display. Inside, the Cancer dog person is a warm, affectionate, and deeply caring person just waiting to hop out of that shell and into your nice, big, safe arms. We think it goes without saying, then, that Cancer dog men and women make exceptionally good parents. They will swathe the little ones with all the attention, affection, and affirmation they have to give. They are also notorious for encouraging any interest their children, or you, might have. Take Rudy, one of our interviewees, for instance. When his daughter,

Lisa, demonstrated an interest in joining the swim team, Rudy had a pool installed that very summer.

Deeply affected by their environment, Cancer dog people are without a doubt the most home-centered of all dog people. Maybe you've seen them pictured in photographs, sitting by a warm blazing hearth, retriever at their feet, pipe in mouth, and a soft blanket gently placed over their laps. Don't be surprised if you're cuddled up watching a rerun of *The Wizard of Oz* and notice the ferverence with which your Cancer dog co-cuddler repeats after Dorothy, "There's no place like home; there's no place like home."

You should also know that these individuals seldom fall in love, but when they do, it is deep and abiding. Emily Brontë's Heathcliffe, tortured by his love for Catherine, was probably a Cancer dog man. When they lose the one they love, it takes years to recover. They like to know you love them, choose them, and desire them above all other people. If you can't provide such attention, then you're in the wrong partnership. If you can, we promise you a very long, loving, and fruitful relationship.

Cancer Bi-nine Person

Let's get a few things straight right off the bat: Unlike the Cancer dog, the Cancer bi-nine carries that shell around, first and foremost, for protection. The Cancer bi-nine is one of the most emotionally fragile of people, and the world seems a cruel and worrisome place. This is why they place such a strong emphasis on having a personal retreat—a safe haven in the advent of storms. Be warned, this bi-nine will see even the most meager rain shower as a torrential downpour.

Some might call bi-nine Cancers paranoid, and, who knows, perhaps they are right. But don't ever tell them that, for calling their bluff will certainly elicit their most paranoid behavior. We're pretty sure that it was a Cancer bi-nine who proclaimed, "Just because you're paranoid, doesn't mean people aren't out to get you."

We interviewed one Cancer bi-nine, Judy, who told us the story of her apartment hunt in New York City. First, she consulted all of her closest friends and family. They believed it was a sound move and agreed she was at a secure place financially. Judy decided to consult her astrologer as well, who informed her that the stars were in a positive configuration for this purchase. Not satisfied, Judy asked her minister what he thought. He, too, thought the idea seemed sound but wondered why she was asking his advice about such a secular matter. At this point, some of her friends suggested she might want to think more about actually looking at apartments, and they jokingly asked her whether she intended to ask her acupuncturist and grocer what they thought of the idea. Naturally, Judy wasn't terribly amused by their comments.

Things proceeded slowly, if surely, and our Judy finally chose a nice one bedroom in the heart of Manhattan. The day the board interviewed her, however, was disastrous. As they grilled her about her finances, requesting income tax returns dating back five years, Judy decided that this wasn't merely an inconvenience to be expected in the course of buying an apartment in New York. Rather, she felt that she had been unfairly singled out for "financial persecution" based on their assessment of her as untrustworthy. We might add that no amount of reasoning by her friends, minister, or astrologer could convince her otherwise. Angered, Judy wrote several scathing and indignant letters to the board, consulted with a lawyer, met frequently with her therapist, and considered hiring an image consultant.

However, as luck would have it, in the midst of all the chaos there happened to sit on the board a fellow Cancer bi-nine, Ben. Luckily for Judy, he seemed to understand her bizarre behavior and actually asked her out to dinner one night. They hit it off immediately, and within one month Judy had painlessly moved into the building; within eight months, Ben had sold his apartment and bought the one next to Judy; within seventeen months, Ben and Judy had gotten married, knocked down the wall separating their apartments, and now live in a spacious two-bedroom apartment.

Judge for yourself, but we believe *cautious* is too bland in describing the Cancer bi-nine personality in all its eccentric splendor; for what should be evident is the unique way in which this bi-nine forges relationships. For Cancer bi-nines, their loved one is that one person in the world who is unequivocally on their side. As a couple, this bi-nine takes "the us against the world" approach, uniting you both in a cocoon of mutual admiration and support. If that sounds at all claustrophobic or insular to you, we suggest you run now, before a Cancer bi-nine manages to entice you into a unique and intriguing web.

Leo Cat Person

Let's just think for a minute about what kind of creature a Leo is. Yes, that's right, it's a big cat, and this is something you dog people and bi-nines out there might want to ponder. The Leo cat person is, in some respects, the cat person's meow, for they are regal, imposing, graceful, and, if provoked, deadly. They are the king of not only the animals, but the hunters, too, and although they bask in the sun like big pussycats, you'd do well to remember the raw power that could be unleashed the moment they roll over, stand up, and decide to pursue.

Astrology

You might have recognized a Leo cat person today. Did you meet anyone with large almond-shaped eyes, thick lashes framing hazel orbs that seemed to be reflecting the sun itself? No matter what color the Leo cat person's eyes are, light emanates from them in unusual ways. Perhaps this person captured and held your gaze longer than usual for a stranger, or maybe you were so intrigued you couldn't look away. No matter, the Leo cat person will smile slyly and think, "Another momentary conquest."

Unfortunately, the Leo cat person's confidence level can border on what some more modest individuals might call arrogance. In fact, perceived arrogance is the one thing that repeatedly gets Leo felines into trouble. They will indignantly argue, "Can we help being decisive, confident, and gutsy? In a world of mice, should we be penalized for daring to be the lions that roar?"

Well, anyone who's ever worked with a Leo boss should know, their reputation as effective and courageous leaders is well deserved. They are usually highly resourceful, charismatic, creative, and determined. Find a Leo cat team leader and you've probably found the winning team. Leo cat people hate to lose; nothing depresses them more. After all, how can they be king of the heap, the undisputed ruler of all they survey, if they're "losers"?

Another important element of the Leo cat personality is the need for social freedom. Therefore, if you tend to be anxious or jealous, this is not the person to make you feel secure. Even though Leo felines rarely cheat, they've been known to purr provocatively at cocktail parties, seducing those around them with that charismatic leonine charm. Just take Jackie O. as an example. Through tragedy and tribulation she maintained her regal bearing, and like a true Leo cat woman, she was always desired and sought after by the gallant and the powerful.

Note that the Leo cat person, although prone to some domineering tendencies, does not want to be surrounded by doormat personalities. Just because they light up when people compliment them does not necessarily mean they want to live life being placated. In fact, because of their unusually high intelligence, they are easily bored by individuals who don't provide some sort of a challenge.

Leo Dog Person

Who's the life of the party? The most successful salesman in your firm? The most glamorous actress at the Oscars? We'll bet you nine to one it's a Leo dog person. These people are indefatigably sociable, overwhelmingly friendly, and incorrigibly direct wherever they go.

Your typical Leo canine will stride into a room, wearing brightly colored body-tailored clothing and expect everyone in the room to stand at attention. These canines know they look good and expect you to appreciate the fact. The truth is, they have an easier time meeting and charming people than those of almost any other sign. Their big, warm smile translates into, "Hi! I was just standing here waiting to meet you!" People just can't seem to resist them, with their sonorous voices, their big bear hugs, and the endearing nicknames they dream up for everyone.

The Leo dog person is also profoundly courageous. Whether it's leaping tall buildings in a single bound, hosting the Academy Awards, or performing any other feat that would leave the average man or woman a shaking bundle of raw nerves, the Leo canine simply smiles through the event with cool and amicable ease. "What's their secret?" many people ask. "How do they keep it all together?" The secret is that they love big events, stardom, fame, and anything larger than life. So go ahead, throw them in the spotlight. You'll get a great performance.

You should also keep in mind that Leo dog people can also be direct to a fault. They hate beating around the bush and would sooner tell you to get lost than to feign interest in what you've got to say. In short, their self-respect causes them to value their time and yours. Although Leos can shoot the breeze with the best of them, they will not foster false illusions or encourage false hope. They like things clear and aboveboard—it keeps the ship running smoothly when everyone is on the same wavelength.

Take, for example, one of the most beloved Leo dog people of all time, Lucille Ball. Always the slightly odd-looking girl with red hair and an overly expressive face, Lucy knew she wanted fame, probably from the time she learned to walk, which is when most Leo dog people realize that walking is merely a prelude to walking onstage. In fact, this person envisions the entire world as a stage, one upon which to shine exuberantly for at least their fifteen minutes. Like Lucy, they are quick to capitalize on what will let them upstage everyone else. Incidentally, if you're performing with a Leo dog person, remember that they have the disconcerting habit of stealing the show. No matter what arena they're in, the Leo dog will, in one way or another, outdo the competition by leaps and bounds.

Leo Bi-nine Person

The Leo bi-nine man or woman is usually a paragon of integrity. The moral and ethical ramifications of any action are always a consideration. So if you want to include them in a scam to rip off the senior citizen's pension funds, don't. Not only will they tell you where to get off, in no uncertain terms, but they will also report you to the appropriate authorities. The Leo bi-nine yearns not only to succeed, but also needs to save the planet, vanquish evil, and reforest South America. Your average Leo bi-nine is wildly ambitious but never ruthless and won't hurt others in the process of realizing a goal. In fact, if these bi-nines can't do it "the right way," they probably won't want to do it at all.

It might be interesting to consider what fuels that superambitious Leo bi-nine personality. If the truth be told, it's a profound fear of failure, which for them means a life of obscurity and no adulation. Two of the successful Leo bi-nines we interviewed are still, after years of analysis, haunted by nightmares in which they either walk onstage to a booing audience or attend an important meeting with no clothes on. Although ambition is a common characteristic of all the Leos, it is most pronounced in the Leo bi-nine. So if you can't get them to relax on vacation, don't forget that failure is simply not an option for these driven people.

Consider Alfred Hitchcock as a case in point. As a director he worked behind the cameras, instead of in front, yet his directed scenes and infamous cameos are even more famous than his actors. You see, even behind the scenes, a Leo bi-nine cannot resist a second or two of celebrity. Most will even settle for notoriety! In a nutshell, the Leo bi-nine is ruggedly individualistic, seeking to carve out a unique niche. We know one woman who, in her efforts to get published, decided to start her own publishing company. She is now the head of her own small but successful feminist press.

When it comes to romance, the bi-nine Leo is highly sought after. Both sexes have an alluring mix of feminine grace and masculine drive, which means that they attract, in equal measure, both sexes simultaneously. If you've just gotten engaged to a Leo bi-nine man, expect men in a sports bar to invite him over to their table for the game *and* for the waitress to eagerly ask if he needs anything else. There's something utterly appealing about the confidence and outward-going nature of these bi-nines.

If it's really possible to reap what one sows, then it's little wonder that Leo bi-nines are successful at every turn.

Virgo Cat Person

If you know a cat person born under the sign of Virgo, you probably know a loner, a perfectionist, and a fierce individualist whose motto is, Perfection first and foremost. Disgusted by slipshod work and with a keen eye for details, a Virgo cat considers life at its best when order defeats chaos. In the workplace, the Virgo cat person can't bear the idea of leading or being led and prefers to work at home or on the road, far from the whims of supervisors or colleagues. Although they dislike depending on others, they can be depended upon, trusted, and meticulous.

They resist trendy clothes, dressing most frequently in a classic style.

When it comes to romance, beware. The cat Virgo knows how to cut losses in the bedroom as well as in the boardroom. If your prospects as a long-term (romantic) investment are low, your Virgo cat person may suddenly kick you to the curb with surprising strength. Virgo felines tend to shun extravagance and loathe conspicuous consumption. It's best to win their heart by pointing out that the expensive gift you gave them was actually on sale. Don't worry, these practical people won't think you're cheap. On the contrary, they will appreciate your thriftiness and pragmatism. Believe us when we say that your sound business acumen will warm their hearts much more than spontaneity or excess ever could.

As terrific as the Virgo cat is, however, we must confess that their perfection-oriented, neat, and finicky ways can become unbearable. For instance, take our Virgo cat friend Hillary, who felt compelled to hang up her date's jacket after he threw it off in a moment of passion. Knowing the amorous moment was broken, Rob just shook his head in frustration. "Hillary, I appreciate that you didn't want my jacket to get creased, but we really need to discuss your obsessive-compulsive ways!" Unfazed, Hillary resumed the amorous pose with admirable gusto, but to no avail. The magic really had dissipated.

Like Cats and Dogs

While you Virgo cat people are hyperventilating about Rob's insensitivity to Hillary, please keep in mind that no one's asking you to become disorganized or slovenly. What we are requesting, though, is that you exercise a modicum of humanity when it comes to affairs of the heart. You may not believe it, but some things really are more important than order—like love.

Virgo Dog Person

The Virgo dog person is extraordinarily hardworking, practical, and, above all, down to earth. Although uninterested in leading, Virgo canines are central to the successful competition of any team's goal. In fact, they love to be needed and are always willing to lend a helping hand. Even though they are decidedly neater and more carefully put together than other dog signs (meaning they know who Donna Karan and Calvin Klein are), these Virgos sometimes own cats to compensate for their sloppier canine tendencies.

Apart from their almost puritanical work ethic, Virgo dog people (like their cat counterparts) are also known for their level-headedness in the arena of romance. In other words, don't expect this canine, however smitten he or she may appear, to indulge your whirlwind fantasies of elopement. These creatures have their feet planted on terra firma, and although one does encounter the occasional Virgo dog flirt or philanderer, most of these folks marry and mate very wisely indeed. In fact, mutual fund investment portfolios may strike them as more romantic than champagne and moonlight. However, should a Virgo ever declare his or her love for you, you can—as Virgos love to say—bank on it.

Interestingly, as stable and centered as these creatures undoubtedly are, they have two weaknesses they rarely disclose: The first is an unhealthy tendency to worry, to be anxious, and to ruminate about impending personal disasters. Secondly, while Virgo dog people may appear together and confident on the outside, they can be a seething hotbed of raw emotion on the inside. Take Barry, for instance, a professional football player who always appeared calm and in control. Unbeknownst to everyone but his wife, he was a compulsive worrier and he suffered from a painful and sometimes debilitating ulcer.

In Barry's words, "People always expect me to be the heart of anything I'm involved in. Take the [football] team as an example. I'm under pressure to boost everyone's spirits, to never look flustered or down, to never show any emotion even when I'm experiencing incredible physical pain....I'm tired of doing it. It's exhausting and frustrating!"

Barry's point is understandable. Who wouldn't be angry at the pressure of always having to be a caretaker?

Like Cats and Dogs

Although Barry eventually found partial relief from his ulcer by practicing yoga and doing special relaxation exercises, Virgo dog people should be aware of their predisposition for slipping into unproductive cycles of worrying. Reasons why they are more vulnerable to this than other astrological or speciel signs are debatable, but we suspect that it's connected to their perfection-oriented, conscientious, and altruistic personality.

Virgo dog people should resist the trap of always having to appear calm, collected, and forever good-natured. People will still appreciate you if you show them that you have weaknesses too!

Virgo Bi-nine Person

At first blush you might assume that the Virgo bi-nine is the most straitlaced of all bi-nines. After all, while other bi-nines revel in openly expressing their unorthodox behavior, this bi-nine appears suspiciously normal. Or, when other bi-nines are busy experimenting with various substances, this odd bi-nine is criticizing the lackadaisical attitude of "irresponsible catnip users," much to the annoyance of their bi-nine brethren. No one knows exactly why this particular bi-nine has turned out so proper, but perhaps the Virgo half of this personality has taken over.

Still, while it's true that the Virgo bi-nine may subtly flaunt bi-nine characteristics, never forget that this individual is not showing everything. It's not that Virgo bi-nines are hiding anything, but as Ralph, our quintessential Virgo bi-nine friend, flatly stated, "Only *I* decide when, how, or with whom I show my true self." In other words, these creatures are true believers in being cautious to a fault and will always hold their cards until the last possible moment. Therefore, refrain from assuming you know them until you've been their close friend for a number of years.

Like many Virgos, these bi-nines aren't known for being especially loquacious, and their reluctance to chitchat is frequently misinterpreted as arrogance. Not that this bi-nine isn't self-confident—they're almost strikingly so sometimes—but conceited they definitely are not. Perhaps the most jarring characteristic of Virgo bi-nines, however, is the ability to see things for what they are. Their willingness to "call it like they see it" often gets them in trouble, but this individual is nothing if not self-righteous while fighting for something they believe in.

Since these people see through pretenses and dishonesty in a millisecond, all bullshit artists should beware: Virgo bi-nines are the least likely people to be charmed by your con. If you're dating a Virgo bi-nine, we suggest that, at least emotionally, you proceed slowly. Since these creatures tend to disclose very little, and aren't the most gregarious folks around, they can seem mysterious, if not intimidating, which they are. The biggest challenge will be in getting your reticent lover to open up and learn to trust. Here's an example of the challenge you're up against. Teresa, acknowledging how difficult it is to date her, admits, "Look, I know that I trust people very slowly and rarely. And for whatever reason I seem to have more defenses than others. This is just who I am, and while it can be frustrating, I promise that when I trust, or love, it really is for a lifetime." There you go. Who can honestly ask for more than that?

Libra Cat Person

If you happen to be socializing in diplomatic circles and meet a highly refined man with impeccable manners who's fluent in three languages and whose reputation as a consummate diplomat precedes him, consider yourself in the presence of your typical Libra cat man. Libra cat people are soft-spoken, tactful, and highly intelligent. They have a knack for gently maneuvering conversations in the direction they wish them to go, while charming anyone they speak to. Yet beware, that facade of amicability and willingness to compromise is not quite as pliant as one might imagine. Remember that underneath all that diplomacy is a will of iron and an agenda more unyielding than their deferential manner indicates. But that's the power of the Libra cat; they get you to think that they're after one thing, and before you know it, you've conceded to their real demands without ever knowing quite how. Just like Scorpio cat people, Libra cat people are masters of strategy. Couple this with a healthy dose of patience, and you can see the Libra cat person coolly waiting for just the right opportunity to pounce. Envisioning life as the ultimate puzzle, this Libra feline is calmly whistling while carefully piecing it together. Never ones to rush, these cats believe that the fun is in the process.

But let's talk for a moment about the legendary sense of justice, which the Libran scales represent, because you'll probably see it manifested most clearly in the Libra cat personality. For these people, the establishment of justice frequently has legal overtones. They love to right a wrong, correct a misperception, or otherwise smooth out wrinkles in the judicial social order. This Libran feline also has a strong sense of duty and responsibility, and once they undertake something, they feel obligated to see it through to the bitter end, no matter how unpleasant the task may be.

Should you decide to move in with your fascinating Libra cat person, please note that he or she is terribly fastidious. For those of you who don't speak the language of order, allow us to translate: They're neat freaks. You may come home and find the apartment repainted, the furniture rearranged, and your clothes replaced. Heed the warning that if a Libra cat person hates your favorite college sweatshirt or your red polka dot dress, you will find that it has simply "disappeared." Later, when you desperately search for the vanished item, your Libra cat friend will look at you aghast and say something seemingly enlightened like, "We must let go of the old in order to embrace the new." In other words, your sweatshirt has been cremated in the nearest incinerator. We strongly recommend hiding anything this roommate doesn't like because in the quest for harmony, these cats are as prepared to sacrifice what you cherish as they are their own belongings. But you can't stay mad for long; they were, after all, just trying to be helpful, and it is hard to lug a lifetime of junk around with you everywhere. In the end, we promise you'll relent and learn to love the harmony Libra cat people can bring into your life.

Libra Dog Person

Typical Libra dog people are complex individuals influenced by both Dionysian (passionate) and Apollonian (rational) tendencies. In their youth they will exhibit a wild side, sowing their oats in true Dionysian fashion. However, this hedonistic side will be tempered by an equally extreme Apollonian side. They might party for two consecutive weeks and then study like monks in their cells for a month. Young Libra canines might get married on Monday and file for divorce on Friday. Not to be confused with the dual nature that Gemini exhibits, the Libra dog individual simply likes to take stock of all possibilities, and reasons the only way of doing so is by going in one direction first, and then the other.

But don't despair, the heady days of youth will give way to a more Apollonian period, much to the relief of family and loved ones, who long ago realized that giving sound advice to the Libra dog person is an exercise in futility. But don't forget, even though they will, over time, cultivate a more balanced approach to life, it does not mean they have necessarily shed all their Dionysian splendor. In fact, if you have yoked your fate to a Libra canine, you might as well get used to a couple of swings here and there. You see, they will never be sure they've achieved harmony and balance unless they periodically tip the scales, just to remind themselves what imbalance feels like.

Take the story of one nice Libra dog man we interviewed who's in his early fifties. Having earned his fortune earlier in life, Gordon now resides comfortably in a quiet suburban town. His wife, a lovely and decisive Taurus cat woman, and his four cat children continue to be frustrated by his inability to make up his mind when it comes to simple things like choosing a vacation spot. Last year, he changed his mind no fewer than three times. First, he booked tickets to Italy, "for the art," then abruptly changed his mind in favor of Scotland, "for the countryside," and then rethought his position on Italy, "such good food and culture." Needless to say, his wife, Cristina, became irate at having to change the plane reservations daily, as well as having to pay stiff airline penalties. Finally, at her wits end, Cristina announced, "The children and I are going to Italy, and if you change your mind again, we will simply go without you." Naturally, Gordon grumbled and continued to discuss the advantages of Ireland and England, but faced with such unequivocal decisiveness, he decided to join them (all the while speculating about what might have awaited them elsewhere).

In love, these charming canines usually leave a string of broken hearts. After the first meeting, they think they're in love, but after a few hours of reflection they realize that perhaps they have been too hasty; those two drinks their date ordered with dinner might mean alcoholism runs in the family. Also, they might not have considered whether or not their mother would like you, or how their second cousin, now residing in Katmandu, might feel about you.

Astrology

Just remember, in their attempt to get the big picture, the Libra dog man or woman sometimes appears to lose sight of you. One dog groomer we interviewed told us about his gregarious Libra canine sister, Sally, who apparently found it hard to refuse a date to the movies while engaged, which left her with a lot of explaining to do when she ran into her fiancé and his sister at the movie theater. Somehow, Sally managed to talk her way out of trouble—they're great talkers, these Libra dog people—and soon both her fiancé and her date were having a friendly drink together, laughing about how this scenario was something out of a sitcom. Incidentally, get ready for numerous episodes of this particular sitcom!

Libra Bi-nine Person

Libra bi-nines are as obsessed with seeking balance as are their Libra dog counterparts, however, the way in which this obsession manifests itself takes a decidedly different turn. The Libra bi-nine believes that the only true path to harmony comes through uncovering life's deeper truths. Frequently, these individuals are well read in Zen Buddhism, Taoism, and other Eastern religions, in addition to Western religions and philosophies. Libra bi-nines are great abstract thinkers. In fact, there must be more theoretical thinkers, like Nietzsche, born under this sign than under any other. The Libra is not, however, intuitive like Pisces, or psychologically perceptive like Scorpios. In fact, if you interrupt them in the middle of a tedious lecture on Freud and ask them to interpret your dream, they may be at a complete loss for words.

It could be said, therefore, that a Libra bi-nine person's life is a study in paradox. Take Billy, a Libra man we met at the dog run, who astounded people by telling them that he hated crowds and public speaking with a passion, then announced he was running for city council. Once you discovered he was a Libra bi-nine, this scenario made much more sense. Billy did hate speaking in public, yet the state of public schools in his community and the increasing crime rate was so upsetting that he felt compelled to take action. Naturally, Billy used his unique brand of logic to reason his way through this: "I *hate* crowds and speaking in front of them, but I love my children and want a safe and intellectually stimulating environment for them to grow up in. Therefore, to ensure that future for them, I must take action. Clearly, public speaking is one aspect of action I must take, and if I like taking action—which I surely do—I must like public speaking!" Presto, once he'd done the logic, Billy embraced speaking at rallies and became a charismatic dynamo.

Astrology

The Libra bi-nine, as you might suspect, also loves debating everything from the right of dog owners to unleash their animals in public parks to the state of peace in the Middle East. Like it or not, these people will seize any chance they get to play devil's advocate and get a good rousing discussion going. What this means is that you might want to pull them aside and forbid them from debating at an important dinner you're having. If you don't, you might find them saying something like, "I bet you're not in favor of the four-day workweek, are you?" to the president of your company, no less.

Their provocative nature can, however, be interesting when it comes to romance. Whoever came up with the adage, Actions speak louder than words, was obviously not courted by a Libra bi-nine.

The Libra bi-nine man, for instance, when smitten by you from a distance, will usually come up and begin a conversation in which he subtly, or not so subtly, convinces you how right you are for him. At first, you may think his dinner invitation is amusing; then you might notice how attractive he is, how well dressed and well mannered, and you might begin to think that perhaps dinner is not such a bad idea. After that, of course, there is no hope for you—you are yet another willing victim of the Libra bi-nine's power of persuasion.

Like Cats and Dogs

Scorpio Cat Person

Beware, cat people born under the sign of Scorpio probably embody the quintessential cat characteristics of being inscrutable, strategic, intelligent, and fastidious.

Let's begin with inscrutability; is it a facade, you ask? Well, yes and no. This cool, calm veneer masks Scorpio's legendary passion, desire, and sting. The Scorpio cat person very consciously creates and monitors an image, which a viewing of any Grace Kelly film will confirm.

Scorpio cat people also place a high value on privacy, and they guard their reputation like a treasured jewel. Scandal, although amusing as a spectator sport, is horrifying if it touches their lives in any way. Speaking of dirty laundry, you should be aware that these felines love secrets, gossip, and rumors, despite what they say. Indeed, they have an uncanny ability to make you tell them your secrets. But don't worry, if you do tell your deepest, darkest secret to a Scorpio cat person, rest assured that after thoroughly analyzing it, this feline will keep it to the grave. The saying that Scorpio cat people listen to everything and reveal virtually nothing is absolutely true. And, if you're fortunate enough to have them confide in you, understand that gaining their trust is a rare and remarkable achievement. Another trick in the Scorpio felines' repertoire is their keen ability to mirror; frequently they are able to retain that admirable inscrutability by effectively reflecting back what the other person is doing or feeling. In this way, they get to know the real you, but the opposite is not true.

Harboring an irrepressible will to dominate and excel, these people hate to lose or submit. Try not to hold their raw ambition against them, for they can also be terrific mentors—as long as your success does not interfere with their power. Also keep in mind that Scorpio cats hate games unless they're playing them, and these seducers have probably played a few in their day. In fact, they are impervious to compliments or insults and can sense insincerity in seconds. So, unless you want to provoke your cat Scorpio into losing control, watch out! This angry feline will surely spend the next nine lives stinging you.

If you do find yourself involved with a Scorpio cat man or woman, bear in mind that underneath that seemingly placid exterior lies a possessive and jealous heart. Don't test your lover's aloof nature by flirting openly with someone else because you'll lose this feline's attention and respect. When a Scorpio feline tells you they love you, which is a very rare occurrence, it means till death do you part, till the end of time, whichever one comes first. When these folks finally do fall in love, it is with passion and intensity; the only problem you may encounter is their reluctance to display this passion and intensity as often as you might like. Still, if you're observant, you'll see fleeting signs of it—the possessive way they hold you at night while sleeping, their biting retort to anyone that criticizes you, their insistence on staying home from work when you're running a 101-degree fever. As for romance, they can do that too, so don't be surprised if on your third anniversary you find the bathtub filled, and roses and champagne in a candlelit bedroom. Who knows, they may even pick you up after work and whisk you away for a weekend in Bermuda. When you insist on going home to pack, they'll assure you that for what they have in mind, you won't need more than what you're wearing. Frankly, there's more than some truth to the myth of the Scorpio feline's obsession with sex.

Scorpio Dog Person

Cautious to a fault, these individuals are frequently mistaken for cat people by virtue of their intense reserve. However, these canines tend to allow their smoldering or, should we say, burning passions to ignite with greater frequency than their cat counterparts. If anything, the Scorpio dog person is dominated by ego. Provocative and suave, they will attract your attention and have no problem keeping it. Not surprisingly, they'll achieve this through the alchemy of aggressive honesty mixed with satiric wit, which is mesmerizing as well as disconcerting. Generally healthy and lithe, these world-savvy people have intense eyes and a very firm handshake. Many people go so far as to call the Scorpio canine strikingly charismatic. Take Katharine Hepburn and Pablo Picasso as examples.

Brave, proud, and courageous, the dog Scorpio, like his or her cat counterpart, is wildly ambitious. However, this dog person—unlike the cat person—prefers the prestige and power of leading a group to working alone. With a burning desire to rule, these individuals head corporations, religious groups, even nations, and they tend to be intimidating and fiercely just.

Visibly powerful and sometimes personally vindictive, we advise against crossing these men or women. If you do, be assured that their vindictive side will take over, and they'll pay you back in kind—with interest added. Take Susan, a Scorpio dog woman we interviewed at a dog show in Manhattan, who was unfairly fired by her first boss, an egomaniacal film producer. Spending the following three years attending production classes and assisting filmmakers, she produced, at the ripe old age of twenty-six, her first independent film, which received a great deal of critical praise. Her continued success increased her power not only in Hollywood but in New York as well. Needless to say, she told the story of her first job experience in great detail to important film executives. Indeed, her ex-boss doesn't know it, but he has been denied funding for several of his films by Susan's friends. It took her a few years, but like most Scorpios in the face of injustice, she had the last laugh.

The flip side to this dark vengefulness is intelligence, intuition, gentleness, and passion. Scorpio dog people, known for their profound loyalty to their friends and loved ones, can be induced to kill if they're convinced a loved one is in mortal danger. And, if you're lucky enough to experience their passion, whether it's spiritual, artistic, or sexual, consider it a rare and wondrous experience.

Scorpio Bi-nine Person

The year 1995 was a hard one for Elizabeth, a Scorpio bi-nine woman we know from graduate school. In February, her mother, whom she was very close to, passed away suddenly. In April, her boyfriend of five years left her for her best friend. Unable to cope with the stress of these combined events, Elizabeth dropped out of her Ph.D. program in psychology at a prestigious university. Hiding from the world at her parents' home, she helped her father deal with his grief and took long walks with her mother's dog,

Jake. Refusing to return the phone calls of even close friends, Elizabeth became reclusive, lost weight, and virtually stopped speaking.

Finally, after four months of this behavior, her father confronted her, saying gently, "Lizzy, your mother died, but you and I are still alive. But because of how you're acting, I feel like I'm mourning my wife and my daughter at the same time." Elizabeth looked away, tears running down her face.

Barely audible, she said, "I guess I'm just not ready to go out and face people. It's hard to pretend I'm having a good time just so other people don't feel uncomfortable seeing my pain. Why is it that people don't know how to deal with grief and death when it's a part of everyone's life?" After a few moments, she mumbled apologetically, "I'm sorry to add to your pain, Dad, but I really need to stay here with you for a while." Elizabeth's words made her father unbearably sad; he decided that maybe time would heal her wounds more effectively than his well-intentioned advice could.

Elizabeth continued living in isolation with her father for eight months. Then, about three weeks after the first anniversary of her mother's death, Elizabeth spent one entire evening sobbing in her father's arms. The next morning, however, brought something unexpected. Her father woke up to the delicious smell of pancakes and sausage and realized that this was the first time since his wife's death that Elizabeth had cooked anything. Entering the kitchen, he was startled to see that she was dressed in a suit, wearing light makeup, and penciling in her weekly schedule. Smiling at her father's surprise, Elizabeth merely said, "It's time for me to move on. I'm ready."

Over the next two months, Elizabeth left her Ph.D. program for good and started working at a family counseling center. Within a year, she founded a support group for people grieving the loss of a parent. Due to her hard work and her ability to empathize and communicate with people, the group became very successful. Her father observed how wonderful it was that Elizabeth had created something that allowed her to both give and receive support from people who understood her pain. She subsequently founded other chapters across the state, and is currently writing about her mother's death to enable other people to let themselves grieve over a loved one's death. Elizabeth's old friends are elated, and her old college roommate, Jill, perhaps best summed up Elizabeth's character in a card that shows a phoenix rising from the ashes; Jill wrote, "To the most courageous and feeling woman I know."

If you know someone who has not only overcome adversity, but turned it to their advantage, chances are it's a Scorpio bi-nine. Resurrection and rebirth are the themes that direct their lives. Whether or not they consciously explore themes of rebirth is irrelevant, for the Scorpio bi-nine feels life's ups and downs intensely and is transformed by it. In that transformation they are ultimately healed, which leads to an ability to heal others as well. Therefore, Scorpio bi-nines are often involved in some aspect of the medical profession, as therapists or counselors, or they write self-help books or work as charismatic faith healers, shamans, or mediums.

If you find yourself in a relationship with one of these people, consider yourself blessed. Scorpio bi-nines are compassionate, empathic, and usually very willing to make a relationship work, often seeking individuals who are sensitive and communicative. So, if you desire a rich emotional life with a rare and altogether special human being, this terrific bi-nine may well be the person for you.

Sagittarius Cat Person

The cat person born under the sign of Sagittarius is supremely ambitious, aiming high and reaching for the brass ring in every endeavor. However, even though you might assume you're dealing with a sophisticated and together cat person, never forget you've also got a Sagittarius on your hands. In other words, say good-bye to some of the finesse we've been telling you is the hallmark of a true-blue cat personality. These felines share that predisposition to bluntness, which so deeply defines the Sagittarius personality, and that's putting it mildly. In brief, you've got yourself an archer whose sharp-tipped arrows are not entirely under his or her control. To be frank, these cat people lack the piercing sting the cat tongue is famous for. While they may be blunt and brutally direct, we can assure you these people are not calculating, particularly strategic, or cruel. We're not quite sure we could say the same for, say, a Scorpio cat person. Furthermore, unlike their astrological cat brethren, these felines detest game playing, deception, and duplicity. If cat people are your thing—but you can't bear to go head-to-head with a manipulative game player—the Sagittarius cat individual may be just your speed.

More openly friendly and physically demonstrative than your typical cat person, this individual is clear-headed, pragmatic, and willing to see the world exactly as it is. With a tendency to being logical, and unlikely to become muddled by mushy romantic feelings, these notoriously blunt archers know exactly what they're thinking—and, like it or not, they will insist on sharing all these thoughts with you. By the way, this person's ability to clearly articulate a medley of complicated thoughts has a fascinating flip side. Your Sagittarius feline may have just explained Einstein's notion of relativity in its entirety to you over dinner, however, when it comes to finding the car keys, or the car itself for that matter, let's just say the original absent-minded professor was surely a Sagittarius cat person.

As everyone knows, Sagittarians are incapable of telling a lie. The cat Sagittarius is no more successful at lying than is their dog or bi-nine counterpart. However, in the cat personality, this characteristic takes a curious twist. Interestingly, since strategy and the careful concealment of emotion is such a cornerstone of the cat personality, this individual will compensate for bluntness by being the least talkative in a professional setting. This means that in business meetings, and at work in general, this feline will simply avoid topics that required dishonesty in any way, shape, or form. Luckily, this individual's creativity, ambition, and razor-sharp mind will ensure a chance for promotion even if the competition can make glib remarks.

When it comes to affairs of the heart, the Sagittarius cat person can be so intense that many a level-headed guy or gal might mistake a fling for something more substantial. Look, these felines take romance seriously, but whether or not they take *you* seriously is a different matter altogether. So, it's best to keep it light until they indicate what their real intentions are. It's worth noting that these creatures love their freedom. So if you have your heart set on marrying one, plan to make quite an effort to get him or her to agree on a definite date for that June wedding you have in mind.

Sagittarius Dog Person

For some inexplicable reason, more dog personalities are born under the sign of Sagittarius than under any other sign, except maybe Aries. And Sagittarius, as we'll have you know, embodies many of the primary dog person characteristics. For starters, they are sincere, open, friendly to a fault. Okay, so they're also a bit clumsy with a distinct tendency to put their foot in their mouth at the most inopportune moment. We suggest these kind-hearted people avoid all aspects of diplomacy. Think about the time you introduced your mother to Bill, your Sagittarius dog lover, and the third thing he said was how sexually compatible you and he were. No sooner had your mother caught her breath than he followed this up with another humdinger. "Gee, Mrs. Stein, you certainly look a lot older in person than you do in your photographs."

Suffice it to say that it was a tedious afternoon for all involved, but after you'd spent the afternoon getting "the look" from your mother, Bill put his arm around your shoulder, turned to your mother, and said warmly, "I can see now where Brenda gets her intelligence, charm, and generosity of spirit. I can't say I'm surprised, after all she's told me about you." Fortunately, things have a remarkable way of turning out all right after a sincere and loving statement like that. But that's the whole point, isn't it? Although your Sagittarius dog lover will, in all likelihood, speak first and spend the rest of the time apologizing and explaining, this individual is truly the epitome of sincerity.

At times like this it is easy to forget that these Sagittarius canines can be emotionally vulnerable due to a certain quality of naïve optimism that they never quite grow out of. This trait means that sometimes they can be taken advantage of, so it's a good thing they're quick to recover and constantly on the move to life's next adventure.

Another lovable trait inherent to these creatures is their fierce loyalty and tendency to become pugilistic if their loved ones are threatened. They cannot bear having their—or your—honor maligned in any way. Just let some unsuspecting party try to sully your name, and you will find out how efficiently the offending party will be subdued. Sagittarius dog people are notorious for bringing their opponents to tears with a few well-placed words.

With a deep desire to help those less fortunate than themselves, these folks have a soft spot for the underdog. Sagittarius dog children are notorious for attacking school bullies and are known for rescuing baby birds, adopting stray animals, and bandaging up younger siblings. Ultimately, this is why you can't help loving them, for even at their most hopelessly blunt and inadvertently offensive, they still have a knack for making everyone feel wanted and cared for.

Generous with their wallets, minds, and hearts, these Sagittarius dog people have retained old girlfriends and boyfriends as their close friends. Then you might realize that in a number of cases those romantic relationships originally dissolved because your wonderful Sagittarius dog person was cheating. These people are incurable flirts, and if a casual flirtation leads in the direction of the bedroom, they're likely, as with everything else, to say yes first and think about you later. But as we've already mentioned, you just can't, and we repeat *can't*, stay angry at this individual. In fact, after a cooling-off period, most exes describe these men and women as incorrigible pups who just can't keep their paws out of the cookie jar.

One last note on these Sagittarius dog people: They're, hands down, the most willing of all dog people to defy the pack instinct when orders or commands from above don't make sense. Frankly, there's nothing easier than spotting the Sagittarius canine in a group—just look for the one who is waving a hand and screaming, "But, why?!" Incidentally, he or she won't stop agitating until an answer that makes sense is provided. It's interesting to note that these keen-minded dog people often end up as the group's trouble shooters. They spot something amiss a mile away and usually end up saving everyone time, money, energy, and embarrassment. It's bizarre to think of a Sagittarius saving anyone embarrassment, isn't it?

Sagittarius Bi-nine Person

Rebellion is the cornerstone of the Sagittarius bi-nine's personality. Like their Sagittarius dog counterparts, these bi-nines gravitate to underdog issues but are more political than the Sagittarius dog person could ever be. For example, this individual is likely to drop everything to campaign for an obscure politician; I bet we could have found a number of Sagittarius bi-nines on the Perot campaign. Ironically, causes are their weakness, for once they find one they can commit to, they follow it with blind devotion. June, a girlfriend of a Sagittarius bi-nine, unflatteringly described this trait as an "addiction," and added, "Once hooked, these people think, live, and breathe their cause—to the point of becoming downright irritating!" Accused of being didactic and dogmatic, they'll expect you to defend their, usually lost, cause right along with them, matching their level of fervor and commitment. If you happen to think it's irrelevant, esoteric, or boring, we suggest you keep that to yourself, lest their slight tendency to paranoia manifests itself in perceiving *you* as the enemy.

Like Cats and Dogs

You should be aware that your typical Sagittarius bi-nine loves to travel and could easily move off to the ends of the earth, remembering at some later date to send you a postcard. We know one Sagittarius bi-nine who left her corporate advertising job and moved to the Sinai Peninsula. She now leads scuba dives in the Red Sea and lives in an adobe desert home with the Bedouin.

The most social of the entire Sagittarius clan, this bi-nine lives to trot around the world, making friends, learning languages, and generally enjoying the vast variety of humanity. If you happen to be dating one of these creatures, just remember, it's not that they don't love you, it's just that they love everything and everyone else too. Hating confined spaces, be they physical or emotional, these people love to socialize, party, and just plain hang out. As a result, there may not be as much "downtime" or "alone-time" with them as you might like, but there's also never a dull moment with these lively folk.

But in the middle of so much socializing, you may wonder how you can tell if you're a Sagittarius bi-nine's special someone. Well, let's just say that the archer is faithful—more faithful than the dog Sagittarius at any rate—and if you're the one he or she comes home to, then you have nothing to worry about. And just in case you're still nervous, keep in mind that the bi-nine Sagittarius has such an abundance of energy that even well after midnight, romance may still be on his or her mind. To keep up with such antics, we strongly advise a catnap in the afternoon.

Capricorn Cat Person

Ambition is the cornerstone of the Capricorn cat personality. These creatures love to work hard and never grumble while paying their dues. But working hard alone is not their sole aim. The Capricorn cat person is driven by the desire to acquire power, and working hard is the surest way to achieve it. You might also find that Capricorn cat people won't take orders for long because the only orders they appreciate are the ones they're giving. So, next time you ask the mailroom clerk his sign and he answers Capricorn, just assume he'll be senior partner within six years.

On the surface, some Capricorn cat people might seem a bit cold and indifferent, but that's only because they're too busy thinking about work or family problems to give you much heed. Unlike the typical cat person, cat people born under this sign sometimes have difficulty separating problems at work from problems at home. Don't be surprised if they bring work home from the office or sacrifice time with you and the family in order to meet deadlines. In most cases, anything that constitutes a problem receives their undivided attention first.

Like Cats and Dogs

Capricorn cat people are realists and materialists; you will hardly ever find them distracted by dreams of wealth or grandeur. Quite frankly, they're too busy achieving the very things other people only fantasize about. Just take Ariel, for example, a woman we met at an upscale pet store in New York City. Ariel started out as a secretary in a large travel agency and soon realized that what she really yearned to do was travel. Therefore, she enrolled in a flight-attendant training program and joined a large international airline. Within two years she had flown virtually every route the airline offered. A favorite among colleagues and frequent fliers, she happened to meet Harold, an affluent New York businessman and Cancer dog person. Enchanted by each other, they soon began dating seriously and were married within a year and a half. Harold was one of New York's most eligible bachelors, and his impending marriage caused quite a stir in the city's more affluent social circles.

Ariel, refusing to be intimidated by the blue-blood matrons of Harold's world, wore a stunning body-hugging white gown to the wedding and disappeared with Harold on their two-month honeymoon. However, when Harold returned his bride did not. In fact, Ariel did not return to his Upper East Side penthouse for several months, her absence causing as much of a stir as her presence had. When Ariel finally appeared after four months, she was unrecognizable. Gone was any trace of social awkwardness or youthful fashion whimsy; she was now an elegant, sophisticated, and immaculately groomed young woman. Instead of becoming the gossiped-about outsider in Harold's social circle, Ariel quickly became the most imitated and sought-after hostess in New York, not to mention one of the most prominent and respected of philanthropists. Just a small example of where a bit of Capricorn cat ambition can take you.

One final note: Capricorn cat people, while unassuming in their demeanor, can harbor quiet depths as well as strategic skill in using your weaknesses against you. In other words, these individuals seek power and can be ruthless in their means of attaining it.

Capricorn Dog Person

The Capricorn dog person is best characterized as a "dog with a bone." *Tenacious* hardly describes the willpower these people possess. Once they set their minds on something, wild horses cannot drag them from the realization of their goal.

Take Dr. Martin Luther King as an example. He not only had a dream, but also had the will and determination to fight racism, even if it meant his own imprisonment and ultimately his life. Now that's perseverance, determination, and commitment—three things the Capricorn dog person knows all about. And, like Dr. King, this person will have a surprising ability to inspire confidence, even in people he or she has only just met.

Possessing strong leadership skills, these canines know how to make decisions and mobilize people. In fact, in almost all cases, you'll find a Capricorn dog person leading the pack. They are the alpha dogs of the human species, so to speak, barking commands and demanding absolute obedience. However, the pecking order will probably mean more to them than just the ability to exercise their very considerable will. Interestingly, Capricorn dog people are deeply invested in both history and tradition and will choose participating in and achieving within an established structure rather than creating their own. Unlike Leos, who love to chart their own course, Capricorn canines are much happier following in the footsteps of great men and women, which is why you will frequently find them in the military, at universities, and in investment banking and law firms. You'll also see them at golf clubs, ivy league clubs—any exclusive institution with a long, rich history.

The Capricorn dog person's interest in tradition also extends to the arts and real estate. These creatures would rather buy the estate of a famous historical figure than constructing one of their own. Relishing antique furniture, books, and art from their favorite historical period, they can spend hours at a Christie's auction. Our friend Jane was married to a Capricorn dog man and complained of being forced to tour the English countryside while her husband excitedly related the history of every single manor house in the region. Luckily, he had made a few acquaintances in the area, through some historical society of course, and he ended up surprising her with a romantic weekend in a charming historic estate.

Capricorn dog people are also very body oriented, reveling in any physical activity that requires endurance, such as long-distance running, mountain climbing, hiking, and triathlons. A word to the wise: Participating in rigorous exercise with these Capricorns will be a surefire way of attracting their attention. They are almost always drawn to individuals who are as highly motivated, intelligent, and physically fit as they are.

Capricorn Bi-nine Person

Capricorn bi-nine men and women are the last people on earth you'd classify as bi-nines. Introverted and shy in youth, they spend a great deal of time worrying about their future security. For some reason, Capricorn bi-nines seem tormented and driven by insecurities. Although harder workers than most people, they never seem to feel entitled to the more joyous and carefree aspects of life. Their youth will be spent juggling a full load of classes and working full-time, already assuming more adult responsibility than their peers. These bi-nines have already determined which profession and college will most effectively facilitate success in their chosen career and are already aware of every innovation and development in their future professional field, even in high school. We hate to say it, but with such a busy career schedule, love comes much later down the line.

Unlike other zodiac signs, the Capricorn bi-nine considers romance as much of a task as everything else. Indeed, marriage for these creatures is only one more goal they must accomplish to ensure their future security. You may have guessed that there will be few whirlwinds or dazzling rendezvous with your bi-nine Capricorn. Instead, these people will want to meet your entire family, compare child-rearing philosophies, and otherwise assure themselves that you are the right person in which to risk a long-term investment. However, like all bi-nines, this one has a quirky feature that makes life so interesting. For these people, that bizarre twist in personality comes with their choice of loved ones. Given their highly conservative outlook, one would expect them to choose a nice safe Taurus dog person, but oddly enough, these highly unspontaneous and risk-averse individuals often fall in love with their opposite—Gemini bi-nines, for instance.

As you can well imagine, oil and water are not as dissimilar as Capricorn and Gemini bi-nines, and these odd-ball astrological combinations seem to work. Much to their amazement, Capricorn bi-nines will veer toward their opposites and somehow end up living happily ever after. Naturally, in a few cases there is heartbreak and heartache on both sides of the crazy love match, but this occurs much less frequently than one might suspect. In fact, one could say Capricorn bi-nine men or women thrive on making the best of what should be the absolutely worst situation, and perhaps herein lies the key to both their success and their appeal.

Aquarius Cat Person

Perhaps you've caught Andrew on a particularly distracted day, and he tells you he's been thinking about selling his apartment and buying a sailboat. "That way, I can just take off on weekends and sail away for weeks in the summer!" You look at this urban New Yorker and laughingly think, What a dreamer he is! But make no mistake, no matter how fantasy oriented these people seem, they are always thinking with more head than heart. In other words, just because an Aquarius cat person has dreams of sailing the Atlantic doesn't mean he hasn't thought about the resale value of his apartment, the cost of a crew, and his chances of winning the World Cup.

Your typical Aquarian feline can't survive without their dreams, but neither can they live without a deep and profound understanding of those dreams. Therefore, you'll find many of these people happily undergoing years of analysis or writing memoirs for every decade of their lives. This tendency can be attributed to the highly critical nature of these men and women. Explanations and answers, which satisfy others, are never quite enough for the Aquarius cat person. The need to understand their life is so profound that often they have an uncanny ability to merge their existential questions with a career. For instance, Langston Hughes, the renowned African-American poet, composed poetry that was lyrical and beautiful, as well as critical, questioning, and provocative. He did not merely write poetry for the sake of aesthetic expression, but regarded it as the record of his highly experimental, artistic, and racially and sexually daring life.

However, once you've gotten yourself into a relationship with one of these felines, you're bound to discover their one tragic flaw: For whatever reason, it is extraordinarily difficult for the Aquarius cat person to trust even those people he or she is closest to. For instance, in the middle of a romantic moment you might look into your girlfriend's eyes and find her not gazing at you adoringly, but assessing you quizzically. This cat person is so guarded and hard to decipher that she finds it hard to believe that you say what you mean or think. If you say, "I love you," she'll ask for a detailed list of the reasons why. If you vaguely answer, "I don't know" to a personal question she's just asked, she will query you to death, convinced that you must be hiding something.

If you desire the attention of such a cat person, simply present yourself as an exciting enigma. She cannot help but respond immediately to mysteries, puzzles, and anything else that piques her highly curious nature. One piece of advice, though: In order to keep the elusive Aquarian attention directed at you, try to find new and interesting ways to present yourself. We suggest you begin reading a classic text such as *A Thousand and One Nights*, which might help you to develop innovative strategies you can use with your Aquarius love.

Aquarius Dog Person

Ever hear anyone say, "I just love getting lost in a crowd"? Well, in all likelihood you were speaking to an Aquarius dog person. They are some of the most gregarious characters you'll encounter, friendly, generous, and willing to have fun at the drop of a hat. Take George Burns, with his warm crinkly eyes, his cigar, and his paternal, indulgent sense of humor, as a prime example. Like all Aquarius dog people, he radiates an aura that is simultaneously good humored, welcoming, and sympathetic; one could truly call him a friend of mankind.

Knowing people's strengths and weaknesses, these folks love to compete and to use their special skills to form an integrated team. In fact, collaboration and cooperation are the cornerstones of these consummate team players.

When it comes to romance, we urge those who seek commitment and monogamy to seek their life partner elsewhere. It's not that we would call Aquarius dog men or women outright philanderers. After all, they're not interested in sexual conquest itself. What these people epitomize is the "free love" generation; they feel that there are several intimate ways of knowing someone who intrigues them, sexuality simply being one of those ways.

Keep in mind that, in general, this sign resents being hemmed in, and this is especially true for the Aquarius dog person in romantic relationships. Both genders envision themselves as free spirits and free agents; consequently, the thought of being accountable to anyone is intolerable. Frankly, the minute you try to "domesticate" their wilder social tendencies, you can be certain that the relationship is on its way to being over. Like the Aquarius cat person, no matter how painful it is, these canines cut their losses when a relationship is no longer fulfilling.

Not surprisingly, this individual makes quite an unusual parent, insisting on seeing children as friends or even as younger siblings. A close friend of ours, Gabrielle, a Capricorn canine, consistently complained that her Aquarius dog mother simply refused to behave like all the other mothers. Instead of demanding obedience and imposing curfews, her mother was a favorite "peer" among Gabrielle's friends and more than happily discussed the merits of premarital sex at the dinner table. Gabrielle found little sympathy from her cohorts when she complained that her mom was more of a best friend than a parent. Interestingly enough, Gabrielle's desire for a more conventional mother diminished with age, and in college she was grateful that she could confide in her mother as a friend.

Generally, this tends to be the way it is with Aquarius dog people; you may bitterly resent their seeming nonchalance in the beginning, but after some time you find yourself appreciating their "live your own life" attitude.

Aquarius Bi-nine Person

Aquarius bi-nine people are the most forward-thinking and future-oriented people in the entire zodiac. When

Like Cats and Dogs

Captain Kirk said, "To boldly go where no man has gone before," he was surely speaking as an Aquarius bi-nine trailblazer (see also his propensity for brief intergalactic affairs and wayward glances at Lieutenant Uhura). You might have noticed that the Star Trek *Enterprise* was more frequently run as a maverick ship, subject more to Kirk's moods and desires, than as a military ship sanctioned by Starfleet Command. Like Kirk, typical Aquarius bi-nines will insist on being pioneers and making up their own rules along the way.

These men and women are idealistic; however, their idealism is typically absolutely their own. In other words, they are not necessarily moved by the dogmas or political convictions of others since their individualism demands that they filter all theories through their own beliefs. Therefore, although they may agree with a certain progressive agenda or a rebel group's cause, all that a cause will ever get from them is perhaps a small donation. Ultimately, the only cult of action these people subscribe to is the cult of self. They intend on marching to the beat of their own drummer and want others to have the same luxury. The controversial actress Vanessa Redgrave is a prime example.

Individualistic and freedom-loving, this person often prefers dreams, ambitions, and thoughts to the company of others, which may account for the number of single

Aquarius bi-nines you'll meet. Sure they've had and have lovers, but there's just something about this bi-nine that prevents them from wanting to settle down. It's not that they're scared of commitment or driven by psychological demons, although some may well be. Rather, it stems from that unique Aquarius bi-nine vision of life. Many have simply decided that marriage or monogamy is not something they believe in, and once they decide something, nothing and no one can convince them otherwise.

We know one Aquarius bi-nine, Colin, who became fascinated by the potential of computer-generated animation while still in high school. He not only loved and collected comics, but was also a cartoonist himself. Majoring in engineering in college, he later founded his own small company specializing in both web-site production and computer animation. When he opened his business, a great many naysayers and pessimists informed him that the Internet was a passing fancy and that independent computer animation would take him nowhere. Being an Aquarius bi-nine, he refused to listen. His company currently not only has one of the most valuable stock options on the market, but is also the premier consultant to a large corporation that specializes in the most technologically sophisticated animation films in the movie industry.

It may take a few years, but one thing is certain when it comes to Aquarius bi-nines. Anything they do today will be in fashion sometime down the line. Whether it's haute couture, technology, or art, you can rely on these people to be the visionaries of their culture.

Pisces Cat Person

Zach was staring at the woman across from him on the subway—the one with shiny jet-black hair and penetrating liquid-brown eyes who looked directly back at him. Today was the day he had decided to ask his boss for a raise, and he was anxious. Yet this mysterious woman with sympathetic eyes seemed to understand the emotional turmoil he was in. The train stopped and she got up. Zach was so compelled that, for the first time in his life, he was tempted to get up and follow her. Gone were his thoughts of job, boss, and salary increase. All he wanted to know was the identity of this woman, whose lingering glance had transformed his day.

He hesitated a moment too long, and she slipped out onto the platform and disappeared. The subway doors closed, and Zach felt trapped by his own inaction. Still, her fleeting presence melted away Zach's fear, and he later demanded a raise from his boss with such self-assurance that he received it immediately. While traveling to Los Angeles on business a few weeks later, Zach intuited something was about to happen. Soon after being seated on the plane, an uncannily familiar woman took the seat next to him. Suddenly realizing it was the woman from the subway, Zach became an immediate believer in fate, destiny, karma—and, of course, in love at first sight.

This is the allure and mystery surrounding the Pisces feline. This individual has the unique ability to look deep into your soul, plumb the depths of your feelings, and to understand the real you. There is frequently a productive pairing between the penetrating Pisces cat and the withholding and dissembling Scorpio dog person. However, Pisces cat people, for all of their penetrating wisdom when it comes to analyzing you, can be surprisingly elusive when you turn your gaze upon them. With a few strokes of that strong Piscean tail, your cat person is soon swimming in different waters.

Constant movement is most important to the Pisces cat person, whose favorite saying is that "still waters run deep, but they also run stagnant." These men and women simply refuse to be caught at the end of anyone's hook. Rather than be captured and held against their element, this slippery cat will simply disappear.

Keep in mind that in order for these people to maintain their inner harmony and complex understanding of the human soul, they will need to retreat periodically. Often they will not be averse to vacationing alone, perhaps spending a few weeks in the desert sleeping under the stars, or maybe renting a cabin in the woods for a month. Wherever the location, and however long the journey, be prepared for this Pisces cat to take off alone and recharge those psychic batteries.

Pisces Dog Person

Let's say you're having one of those days when nothing seems to go right. You've spilled coffee on your boss, lost an important invoice, and forgotten your briefcase. Just when you're ready to scream in frustration, your co-worker Margaret ambles along. Sensing you're frazzled, she sits down, and soon you're relating the day's disastrous events to her. Smiling broadly, Margaret tells you about the time she ruined the CEO's dinner party by having steak dinners catered to a group of vegetarians. Soon you realize that you're actually laughing, and Margaret is wandering off to the photocopy machine. Chances are, your friendly listener, Margaret, was a Pisces dog woman.

Pisces dog people are best described as easygoing, relaxed, and flexible. In fact, of all the signs in the cat, dog, and bi-nine zodiac, the Pisces dog person, in particular, has to rank as the most capable of giving unconditional love. Have you broken your diet more times than you can remember? Perhaps you just can't give up hope on that married man you've been seeing for a year? Well, you can bet your bottom dollar that even if all your other friends have declared a moratorium on the topic of dieting or married men, there is one place your repetitive conversation topics will not be shunned, and that is at the home of your good Pisces dog friend. Not only are these canines sympathetic and empathic listeners like Margaret, but they also tend to be in tune with the subtle distress signals that people around them send. This is probably why some people describe them as clairvoyant.

Unlike Aries or Leo dog people, Pisces canines aren't trying to change the world, make a fortune, or otherwise bend destiny to their iron will. To begin with, rigid and inflexible things are anathema to their character. In other words, these people are tender hearted and deeply emotional; for instance, call a Pisces man a cruel name and he'll ask you why you're trying to hurt his feelings. After all, in his world no one would willingly hurt someone else. One word of warning; don't mistake his good-naturedness for a lack of intelligence, or you may find yourself the target of a rather uncomfortable character inventory in front of your friends at the local bar.

Finally, remember that these canines put a great deal of stock in their highly developed sense of intuition. Many of them will tell you they live solely by intuition, and they're not exaggerating. Consequently, a standard response you can expect from them when asked if they feel like doing a particular thing is, "Somehow, this just doesn't feel right," or even, "I'm not getting the right vibe." You'd be wise to heed their sixth sense.

Pisces Bi-nine Person

When a Taurus declares that to forgive is divine, the Pisces bi-nine will claim that to suffer is sublime. Not to be confused with masochists who seek out their own subjugation, Pisces bi-nines simply experience the ups and downs of the world with more intensity than the rest of us. For instance, there's Gail, a woman we met browsing through the pet section at Barnes and Noble, who is a dreamy, dewy-eyed poet who sacrificed everything for her art, living in a tiny room on coffee, a can of tuna, and two slices of bread a day, a portion of which goes to the stray cat who keeps her company. Then there's Carla, the physician in the emergency room who treats fatal gunshot wounds every day and still sheds tears every time she loses a patient. We can't forget Carlos, a man we interviewed in Chicago, who's a public school teacher who tirelessly gives of himself at an urban high school where students have virtually no resources available to them. Finally, there's Amanda, the adolescent girl whose thespian soul is crushed because her father is demanding that she major in economics and pursue a master's in business. As you can see, the Pisces bi-nine is not entirely of this world, always marching to the beat of a different, and far more sensitive, drummer than the rest of us. Indeed, maybe picturing your Pisces bi-nine as living on a frequency you cannot access will go a long way in explaining this unique and quirky individual.

Both Pisces bi-nine men and women have a decidedly dark side. Their emotional sensitivity makes them susceptible to melancholy and downright moodiness. Known for throwing their fate into the hands of destiny, you'll hear them saying things like, "Well, it's in the hands of the universe now." They love to see where the current is taking them, rather than charting their own course. However, if the seas get too rough or their sailboat overturns, just watch how quickly that gentle and sunny Pisces bi-nine demeanor evaporates. If destiny deals them an unpleasant hand, these bi-nines will snap irritably, lapse into days of sullen silence, or simply spiral downward into a psychological breakdown or a frightening depression.

Averse to structure and senseless convention, these bi-nines believe that doing something "because we've always done it that way" is never a good enough reason. Strong believers in, and practitioners of, esoteric mysticism and psychic phenomena, this bi-nine is hardly ever impressed by objectivity and the scientific method. Don't be surprised if you have a migraine and your Pisces bi-nine sister sends you to the acupuncturist. These Pisces have a tendency to swear by the merits of Eastern and holistic medicine. After all, they'll point out that the mysteries of the universe or even curing the common cold still haven't been accounted for by Western science.

Most Pisces bi-nines simply wait for a positive and strong current to carry them back up into the good fortunes of daily life. Although one usually comes along, there are the less fortunate ones who feel fated to remain depressed, unhappy, and unsuccessful for years. But if they manage to find a strong partner who helps smooth the road for them, their moodier side can be alleviated altogether. Should this occur, you'll be left with a happy-go-lucky dreamer who utilizes creative talents to commit random acts of beauty in the world. So, if you're in the mood for an interesting and unpredictable ride, yoke your fortune to a Pisces bi-nine; otherwise, let us recommend someone more staid, such as a Capricorn dog person.

CHAPTER 6

Common Sense Wisdom for the Cat, Dog, and Bi-nine Personality

All I Really Needed to Know I Learned in the Litter: Canine Observations about Ordinary Things

Dog people, occasionally accused of not being as introspective as they might be, may have failed to realize that certain rules of puppy behavior are *directly* applicable to them in their canine-centered lives. The following is a list of eleven rules that puppies master in the litter, and it could be argued that these simple axioms contain all the wisdom every dog man and dog woman need to live a happy and fulfilled life.

Like Cats and Dogs

1. Remember, you're the pick of the litter.

This adage stresses the importance of having self-esteem throughout your life. It doesn't matter if you're picked last for the football team, if your sibling always does things better than you do, or if your boss promoted someone else. Remember, no matter what anyone says, *you* have worth and you are the pick of the litter!

2. Don't forget that, as Diana Ross sang, "You can't hurry (puppy) love."

Sometimes dog people, like everyone, try to rush love and romance, thinking that if they don't, they'll never find a partner. This is a gentle reminder that love happens in its own time... and it will happen.

3. Anyone with a hang-dog expression or with their tail between their legs deserves a hug.

This teaches empathy and sensitivity. Dog people need to be kind when they see other dog, cat, or bi-nine people in pain.

4. Your happiest days were being a puppy in the litter.

This nostalgic axiom stresses the importance of family, siblings, and warmth in all our lives. Essentially, it's a harkening back to those halcyon days.

5. Let your bark be worse than your bite.

Use words instead of fists when settling an argument. This is especially important for male and female dog children who have a reputation for excessive roughhousing. This also applies to some dog men who, in their adolescence, choose to settle fights physically, instead of talking it out rationally.

6. Don't waste time barking up the wrong tree.

This speaks to the futility of engaging in any exercise that doesn't yield results. Of course, it may apply to a diversity of things but is especially useful to remember at work and in affairs of the heart.

7. Never engage in the expression, It's a dog's life.

Obviously, this is a self-deprecating statement that directly violates our maxim of thinking of ourselves as the pick of the litter.

8. Don't soil the home.

Okay, so this is an upscale way to describe housebreaking puppies, but this can be translated to mean that dog people need to be discerning about what they bring into their homes and therefore into their lives. As we know, there are several ways to "soil" one's home and disrupt one's household, such as lying to your partner and children, having an affair, or indulging an addiction.

9. Don't bite the hand that feeds you.

Meant both figuratively and literally! Sometimes dog people lose the bigger picture in a minor conflict, so remember that screaming at your boss, while cathartic, will not prove to be in your best interests when paycheck time rolls around.

10. Remember, it can be a dog-eat-dog world.

Dog people, due to their trusting and sometimes slightly naïve nature, need to be cautioned—more than cat or bi-nine individuals—that it can be a harsh world. They need to be particularly wary of being taken in by certain unscrupulous cat and bi-nine individuals seeking to take advantage of them.

11. Be your own dog.

Made famous by Red Dog beer, this phrase underscores the importance of always being an individual, a nonconformist, and your own person.

Chicken Soup for the
Bi-nine Soul

Bi-nine Boy Faces Dog-Eat-Dog World

Marty was so terrified he couldn't move. He stared at all the other junior high school students who appeared so relaxed, confident, and happy on their first day of school. Having recently moved into the area with his family, Marty hadn't had a chance to make any friends. Worse yet, he was painfully shy and had a tendency to stutter when he felt anxious. He vowed to himself that no matter what, he wouldn't stutter in front of the other kids today.

From the corner of his eye, Marty observed his gregarious older brother, Steve, already making friends. Steve made it look so easy, with his social dog-man-personality skills and handsome face, that Marty sometimes wondered how they could be so different. Luckily, he and Steve were close, and Marty loved knowing that he could always count on his big brother for help if necessary. Marty slumped his shoulders, shoved his hands into his pockets, took a deep breath, and walked up the steps of Williams High School.

The first two months were a nightmare for Marty. Although his grades were exceptionally high and his teachers wrote glowing reports on all his papers, Marty still couldn't seem to fit in. He just didn't want any part of the ordinary world of junior high boys—with their pretense of being macho, their tendency to roughhouse, their general immaturity, and their interest in heavy metal rock groups.

Steve, of course, had easily made it onto the varsity football squad and became one of the most popular guys at school. Suddenly, it seemed as though Steve just didn't have time for Marty. Fiercely social, Steve relished hanging out with his new friends and his girlfriend, and while Marty missed him intensely, he pretended that he was happy in front of Steve.

As Marty became more and more introverted, he started retreating into literature, voraciously consuming book after book. He loved how easy it was to explore other worlds just by opening up a new book. Then, one day he decided to compose poetry. Marty was amazed at how natural it felt for him to write and by how fluidly the words came out of him. He decided to send his first poem, which was about a bi-nine boy finding his real self in the midst of a cat-and-dog-centered world, anonymously to the school paper. To his surprise, they published it! During that school year, the school paper published no fewer than eight of his poems. Soon everyone at school was trying to figure out who this gifted mystery writer was.

Finally, at the end of the school year, Marty decided to attend an awards ceremony so he could see his brother receive a varsity letter for excellence as the quarterback on the football team. Suddenly, Marty heard Dr. Bender, the respected head of the English department, announce that the mystery poem writer had won the prestigious writing award and would he or she please come up to the podium to accept it.

Waves of nausea overcame Marty, but he managed to stumble up to the podium, aware of the stunned faces of all those around him. He couldn't blame people for being shocked; after all, it was unusual for an eighth grader to win an award usually reserved for a high school senior. Blushing as he heard the glowing praise from Dr. Bender, Marty wasn't sure what to say as she handed him the engraved plaque. Deciding it would be appropriate to recite the last four lines of the very first poem he had submitted to the paper, Marty steadied his voice and said:

> *The dog soul follows the canine way,*
> *And the cat soul seeks the feline,*
> *And in between, in the sultry gray,*
> *There thrives the enigma we call bi-nine!*

Greeted by thunderous applause, Marty no longer felt frightened standing in front of so many of his teachers and peers. He choked up as he saw Steve gazing proudly at him, and tears came to Marty's eyes when Steve rose from his seat to give him a standing ovation.

Two Stupid Things Felines Do
to Mess Up Their Lives

STUPID COMMITMENT PHOBIA: When *commitment* is a four-letter word. *Scared to love, you repeatedly lie to yourself and others about where the real problem lies.*

Remember Katie, the commitment-phobic cat woman? This chapter is dedicated to her and all cat women and cat men who, for some reason, are more commitment phobic than dog people or bi-nines.

Scared of Commitment Means *You*
Have an Issue, Not the Other Person

Katie represents many felines when she confesses that the most terrifying word in the English language for her is *commitment*. Why this seemingly innocuous word conjures up a jail sentence for so many cat people seems bizarre to canines and bi-nines who accuse felines of being absurdly claustrophobic. Yet, this feeling of being fenced in, suffocated, and trapped is very real to the true-blue cat personality who fears any encroachment on physical and emotional boundaries.

It is imperative for cat people to realize, however, that it is unkind, not to mention incorrect, to blame their unsuspecting canine or bi-nine partner of trying to suffocate them. Should a cat individual, like Katie, choose a lifestyle in which she or he feels genuinely fulfilled *not being* in a traditionally defined and committed relationship—well and good. But, cat people, listen up; Accusing your canine or bi-nine partner of purposefully attempting to curtail your precious sense of freedom is blatantly unfair. It's vital for felines to understand that this issue is about them, *not* about the other person.

You Don't Need a Ph.D. in Commitment to Figure It Out

The truth is that once cat people accept the need to be honest about their commitment phobia in an intimate relationship, they'll find many canines and bi-nines genuinely interested in finding an alternative arrangement that suits both parties. For instance, the photojournalist that Katie finally ended up dating was a classic bi-nine who was willing to be flexible in a relationship. Therefore, the reason that their relationship ultimately worked was because Katie was able to articulate her boundaries to him in a way that she never could with her first boyfriend. Why? Because Katie herself hadn't fully understood what was happening and what her own needs were.

Essentially, we're saying that with self-understanding, everything is possible. If cat people with commitment issues date individuals who are able to respect their intense

Like Cats and Dogs

desire for privacy and freedom, a mutually beneficial relationship is possible. We would like to remind all felines, however, that making a feline-canine relationship work for the long haul can sometimes be very challenging. This is because most dog people seem almost genetically programmed to be social. After all, who can blame them? Unlike cats, dogs are governed by their natural pack instinct.

Dare to Be Vulnerable

Remember when Katie's boyfriend was both irritated and confused by her actions? It was because she couldn't explain why she was feeling suffocated by the thought of moving in together. He had assumed she was just removed and disinterested when, in fact, Katie was experiencing a lot of painful emotions. Cat people, like their animal counterparts, are often perceived as being guarded and aloof. While cat individuals like Katie present a cool and together exterior, they are often a hotbed of turbulent emotion on the inside. Unfortunately, they rarely let anyone see their true feelings.

While Katie decided that she needed to be with a different kind of man, other cat people might occasionally try letting their guard down, as difficult and unnatural as that may feel. Doing so will allow them to reveal all those fascinating and hidden aspects of their personality that can enable their partner to understand them better. In short, being vulnerable, for better or for worse, is simply an indelible part of love, and the key to making a relationship work. If cat people can dare to be vulnerable, they might be pleasantly surprised by the beauty they find in the outside world as well as inside themselves.

STUPID BRILLIANCE: "Using the power of my intellect, I can control virtually anything." *Overly strategic and intellectual, you can't appreciate something unless you overanalyze and control it.*

Who can forget John, the overly strategic cat man who had the world at his fingertips but lost the woman of his dreams, all because he couldn't stop playing head games with her, and himself. More than a few cat men and cat women around the world have been accused of being overly manipulative and shrewd. While many cat people are angered by this stereotype, we must admit that there is a tendency for *some* cat individuals, of both genders, to be obsessive about attempting to control every event and person in their life.

Win the Battle, Lose the War

We talked with John recently, and believe it or not, he is still puzzled as to why Jennifer stormed out the door yelling, "Love is not a chess game!" This incident is tragic not only because John genuinely cared for Jennifer, but also because, at a crucial moment, John proved incapable of admitting to, and being honest about, a significant part of his personality. The point here is that unfortunately John wasn't able to make the distinction between manipulating a business situation and participating in an intimate relationship. In short, since John treated Jennifer as another winning move—another trophy—he succeeded only in objectifying her in the most humiliating way possible. And since Jennifer knew his game, she was repulsed enough to walk out the door.

Look, cat people, you are profoundly intellectual and have a genius for strategy; it's a wonderful gift. But let John be your example—inappropriate strategizing can be lethal to your love relationships! Ask John, if you don't believe us. He'll tell you.

You Have to Live Life with Your Heart, Not Only with Your Head

In short, all we're saying is that in order to have a meaningful life, it is necessary to strike a balance between your head and your heart. Consider the plight of a cat woman we interviewed, Jody, who told us that even though she tried not to be too cerebral in her love life, she just couldn't stop overprocessing every single thing that happened between her and her lover. A consummate bridge player,

Jody acknowledged that before making any move in her personal life, she considered *all* the possible consequences. She claims that not analyzing the moves painstakingly and meticulously makes her feel terribly insecure and powerless.

Ironically, obsessing about being in control can sometimes produce the opposite effect. It may be a constructive exercise for cat people to set aside a few moments each day and consciously experiment feeling comfortable *not* being in control of a situation. While it may initially make you feel insecure, it is essential to feel comfortable in ambiguity and vulnerability.

Even Bobby Fischer Doesn't Play Chess
Twenty-four Hours a Day

For you die-hard cat individuals who are outraged by our suggestion of *voluntarily* not being in control of every situation, all we can say is that even one of the greatest strategizers in the history of chess, Bobby Fischer, didn't play the game twenty-four hours a day. Obviously, we mean this statement more than just literally!

If you don't believe us, consider John's situation again; although he's young, attractive, and enormously successful, he's doomed to spend eternity being fixated on controlling—doing things only for the sake of winning and achieving. Not only is it just plain exhausting, but more important, how can it be fulfilling to live one's *entire* life in this manner? The truth is that living this way may feel safe, but in reality it is hollow; it's profitable in some respects maybe, but unfulfilling on the deeper emotional levels.

If you cat people can manage to temper the obsessive controlling with emotional spontaneity and vulnerability, you won't be saying what John said after he realized that Jennifer was gone for good: "Well, looks like this time I won the battle but lost the war. I guess it wasn't really worth it, after all."

Dogs Are from Pluto, Cats Are from Saturn

Have you ever suspected that cats are from Saturn and dogs are from Pluto? Many moons ago in the cat kingdom of Saturn there was an uprising, a stirring in the air that no kitten or cat could account for. Oddly, many members of this all-cat community were having the same dream about creatures who, like them, possessed tails and four legs but who tended, on the whole, to be an entirely different species. The cats flicked their tails at their local meow mixers and considered the possibility of these fascinating creatures existing in more than just their minds.

And then it happened. One day one of these creatures (who called himself a "dog") entered their lives. He informed the cats that he was the diplomat of the dog kingdom of Pluto and had a confession: Powerful satellites had been observing Saturn for several months now, and consequently, many puppies and dogs in Pluto had become besotted by these exotic creatures.

After the various dog and cat heads of state met, it was decided that all interested cats and dogs (and there were many) were to immigrate to another planet for an altogether new beginning. And so it was.

On Earth, however, something went terribly askew. Many dogs and cats seemed to forget the power of mutual attraction that had brought them there in the first place, and they started fighting, as the oft-quoted saying goes, like cats and dogs. This chapter is one attempt to bridge the enormous chasm that has developed since that moment.

Cats and Dogs: Their Differing Expressions of Intimacy and Love

If only we had a dime for every time an exasperated cat or dog person shrugged their haunches and screamed, "But what do cats/dogs *really* want?!" This section will attempt to bridge what is perhaps the biggest gap between dogs and cats: their differing needs for intimacy and love.

We've emphasized that one enormous difference between most dog and cat individuals is the value canines place on interacting with the world, while felines favor the world within. To elaborate, canine personalities are, in virtually every way, interested in engaging in highly social ways. Cats, on the other hand, are notorious for being so private they can seem cold or aloof.

The romantic implications of this difference for a cat and dog couple is enormous. For instance, Carol, a woman we interviewed at Petco, is a vibrant dog person who enjoys watching erotic films on the VCR with her slightly repressed cat boyfriend, Lawrence. She decided not to give him the traditional tie on Valentine's Day but, instead, wanted to surprise him by renting an erotic film and by buying some titillating lingerie at Victoria's Secret.

Feeling overwhelmed by the enormous range of erotica at the video shop, she called up her best girlfriend, Leah (who also happened to be Lawrence's older sister), and Craig, an old boyfriend, and begged them to join her so they could help her select the most sensual video. After much lively debate, all three friends decided unanimously that *Unleashed Ardor* looked like the most promising. Thrilled by the prospect of unleashing her own ardor, Carol asked her friends if they would accompany her to Victoria's Secret since they had proven so helpful with the video selection. Again, after conversing vigorously, they decided on an appropriately sexy nighttime outfit for Carol. Carol smiled gratefully at her friends, glanced at her watch, and announced, "The countdown has begun. Only three and a half hours more."

That evening, Carol was absolutely blissful. Lawrence had surprised her with an exquisitely cooked Italian meal and some wonderful wine. Best of all, he loved her lingerie and was enjoying *Unleashed Ardor*. As they started to kiss passionately, Carol couldn't contain her excitement and whispered, "We just knew you'd like it."

Lawrence stiffened and said, "We?"

"Oh, just Leah and Craig, it's nothing."

Lawrence abruptly sat up and looked aghast. "You mean you picked this video out with my sister and your ex-boyfriend? Are you crazy?"

"What's wrong?" asked Carol, genuinely perplexed. "The selection was so huge at the video shop and Victoria's Secret, and I really needed a second opinion."

Lawrence's eyes widened. "They went with you to pick out the lingerie too? Why didn't you just invite all your co-workers as well?"

Ignoring his sarcasm Carol retorted, "I did, but they were all busy. God, you are uptight!"

"Me, uptight? That's not the problem....Carol, is nothing sacred to you?!"

At this point, both Carol and Lawrence realized they were at an impasse. Weeks later, an enlightened bi-nine counselor, Harry, spoke at length to Lawrence and Carol about the incident. Summarizing, Harry said that Carol couldn't understand what Lawrence could possibly mean by asking her if nothing was sacred, while Lawrence was astonished that Carol had the gall to ask his sister and her ex-boyfriend's advice in buying (what he considered) very intimate and private items. And this, declared Harry, is precisely where the problem lay.

You see, for Lawrence, a classic cat man, sexuality is a very private, intimate, and sacred space, to be talked about and experienced only with one's lover. That's what makes it special for him. Carol, however, has an entirely different conception of sexuality. For her, nothing is so sacred that she doesn't feel comfortable discussing it with her friends. Keep in mind, though, she's a highly social and pack-oriented dog person. Therefore, for Carol to discuss sexuality, frankly and openly, with her very close friends does nothing to make it any less private, intimate, or special for her. On the contrary, according to Carol, sharing her experiences with close friends often enables her to better appreciate and understand the intimacy she shares with her lover.

You'll be happy to know that Lawrence and Carol have not broken up and are trying to better understand each other's actions. Although you can be sure that they will continue to surprise each other with their differing attitudes and actions, Lawrence and Carol have understood a few vital things about love between cat and dog people: Carol has learned that the privacy and quietude that cat people seek is an entirely appropriate response to the way they structure their world, while Lawrence has grasped that going outside of one's intimate relationship is both beneficial and necessary for the worldly dog individual.

Dog-Cat Dictionary

This section examines eight key terms used by cat and dog people with the goal of providing felines with an intimate understanding of canine culture, and vice-versa.

1. CURIOSITY KILLED THE CAT. Many people around the world and through the centuries have wondered why the expression "curiosity killed the cat" refers so explicitly to a cat. After all, why isn't the phrase "curiosity killed the dog" ever used? The reason, quite simply, is that cats, and by extension cat people, are undoubtedly the most curious creatures you'll ever encounter.

Even as boys and girls, cat individuals are obsessed by an intense desire to investigate and learn, which is markedly different from most children's desire to explore. The key difference is that after several years, most children outgrow the fixation of having to know the "why" of everything. Cat people, however, often sustain their inquisitive interests even into adulthood and pursue careers like archaeology, psychiatry, or private investigating so that they can continue to explore the worlds that fascinate them so much. One cat woman detective, acknowledging the danger inherent to her line of work, commented, "Okay, curiosity might kill the cat," and then countered, "but don't forget we felines have nine lives!"

2. SEX KITTEN. The dictionary defines this term as "a woman with conspicuous sex appeal." We believe that an important way to supplement this definition is to make a reference to the Catwoman character in *Batman*, since she is the living embodiment of a sex kitten. The reasons why one woman would be described as being more seductive than another woman are more complex than you might suspect. In order to qualify as a sex kitten you must exude feline sensuality and grace. It's not so much the symmetry of a woman's features as it is the aura of her potential sensuality that makes all the difference. A sex kitten is the woman who can make giving a speech, peeling an onion, or going rock climbing an erotically charged experience. These women exude, at any age, a youthful joie de sexual vivre unparalleled by other women.

One popular myth is that sex kittens are so named because they engage in sexual activity with great frequency. Not at all! The sex is placed in front of *kitten* only because of the tremendous sexual *appeal* that these women have. Famous sex kittens past and present include Marilyn Monroe, Rita Hayworth, Goldie Hawn, Julia Roberts, Alicia Silverstone, Heather Locklear, and, of course, Eartha Kitt in the original *Batman* series.

3. CATNIP. *Webster's Collegiate Dictionary*, ninth edition, describes this as a "strong-scented mint (*Nepeta cataria*) that has whorls of small pale flowers in terminal spikes and contains a substance attractive to cats." In layman's terms, this includes any substance that enhances the physical and psychic pleasure of an event. And let's face it, given how uptight cat people can be, a little herbal relaxant may not be such a bad idea; it's certainly a favorite among the bi-nine population.

4. CAT BURGLAR. It is interesting that W. S. Gilbert wrote, "With catlike tread, upon our prey we steal" because this phrase perfectly captures the *modus operandi* of a cat burglar. While cats have objected for years that the pejorative word *burglar* is sullying their good name, it may be of some comfort for them to learn that a cat burglar is certainly no ordinary thief.

The dictionary asserts that a cat burglar is "especially adept at entering and leaving the burglarized place without attracting notice." This definition, it must be said, is omitting a vital point: With their all-black costumes and their sleek and limber bodies, cat burglars have raised stealing to a veritable art form! And it goes without saying that whatever activity (dubious or not) cat people engage in, if they don't want to be caught, chances are they probably won't be.

5. PUPPY LOVE. This term, first recorded in 1834, is defined as being only a "transitory affection" between adolescents. It must be argued that this summation diminishes the true importance of this wonderful event. While puppy love may not have the longevity of romantic love experienced later in life, it does mark the *first* time in a person's life that they experience romantic love at all. And, as we all know, often it's a momentous event. In retrospect, it sometimes appears that puppy love is the best kind of love, because the person going through it is too inexperienced to realize the real complexities and work that mature love entails.

6. DOG-EAT-DOG WORLD. It is ironic that this phrase means "marked by ruthless self-interest" when this is the characteristic least associated with dog people. We first touched upon this negative expression in our section All I Needed to Know I Learned in the Litter when we cautioned overly trusting dog individuals to beware of people who may not seek to work in their best interests.

What is fascinating about this term, though, is that it clearly indicates that the world must have no real understanding of the dog persona. Saying that dog people are ruthlessly self-interested is like saying that cat people are the most gregarious and social creatures you've ever met. It's quite absurd.

According to *Webster's Dictionary*, this adjective came into existence in 1834, and, rest assured, we are committed to finding the misguided individuals, probably cat people, who created this highly inappropriate and insulting term.

7. DOG IN THE MANGER. This fascinating phrase was first used in 1573, emerging from a fable about a dog who stopped an ox from eating the hay that he himself did not want. Thus, the meaning of this is "a person who selfishly withholds from others something useless to himself." As far as actual dog people are concerned, there is frequently a misunderstanding regarding their actions. Dog people do not necessarily care about the "hay" so much as they can be highly protective and guarded about what's theirs. Again, much like the phrase dog-eat-dog world, this one is highly unflattering, and we find it preposterous that it has come into being at all. We do, however, urge dogs to examine some of their more territorial impulses.

8. TAIL BETWEEN YOUR LEGS. How many people stop to consider the significance of a dog's tail? We wager, not

many, which is unfortunate because a dog's tail can indicate virtually everything about his or her mental state. If
the tail is up and wagging to and fro, you can bet the dog is
excited, self-confident, and feeling a certain doggie joie de
vivre. Conversely, should a dog's tail be drooping between
his legs, you can be sure that your dog is experiencing
some sort of canine sadness and depression. Likewise,
humans who have their "tail" between their legs, figuratively speaking of course, are also depressed and usually
feeling submissive or even cowardly. If someone accuses
you of having your tail between your legs, understand that
you are being subtly insulted and try and do something
proactive to change your attitude from one of submis-
sion—to optimism.

CHAPTER 7

Understanding Your Cat, Dog, or Bi-nine Lover

The most common complaint we hear from cat, dog, and bi-nine people is that they just can't understand why their interspeciel partner reacts so differently from the way they do. Each party feels that his or her response is the normal, correct, or best one, and this is precisely where the difficulty arises.

For instance, bi-nine and cat people are often critical of three things about dog people: They resent how "expressively" dog people vent their anger, they are irritated by how slovenly some dog persons can be, and, finally, they are frustrated at the difficulty dog individuals have in separating their work (public space) from their family (private space).

Dog and bi-nine people are frequently perplexed by how aloof cat people act even in relation to loved ones, how fastidious and controlling they can be when it comes to household chores, and finally how cat people insist on keeping some parts of their life discreet.

Finally, dog and cat people alike are offended by the "superiority complex" many bi-nines have toward them, they are concerned by how little the bi-nine cares about maintaining or giving any impression of normalcy, and finally they are appalled by the bi-nine's laissez-faire attitude toward experimentation—whether this means with mind-altering drugs, sexuality, or with anything deemed radically different from the mainstream.

This section will explore these dog, cat, and bi-nine personality flaws expressly for the benefit of your lover with the hope that it will enable your significant other to better understand, and maybe even appreciate your, shall we say, idiosyncrasies.

Understanding Your Dog Lover

When confronted by your angry dog lover, how should you react? First of all, be prepared for a fireworks display in terms of emotions, and remember that it is natural to the dog personality to vent in precisely this dramatic fashion.

Understanding Your Cat, Dog, or Bi-nine Lover

It may be helpful to keep in mind that dog people express their anger in an explosive and forthright manner, while bi-nines and cat men are sometimes guilty of avoiding anger and confrontation altogether.

In order to more fully appreciate the differences between these divergent reactions to anger, it becomes essential to understand that explosive anger is exactly what it seems to be: Out of the blue, the dog personality is triggered by something and erupts like a volcano. Anger avoiders, however, function a great deal more subtly. Feeling tremendous guilt about their anger, bi-nine and cat men sometimes believe that it might be too frightening for themselves (or anyone else) to face their true rage, so they simply pretend everything is okay.

Considering these wildly opposing ways of dealing with anger, it is evident that cat, bi-nine, and dog persons need to come to some agreement about how they will deal with this turbulent emotion in their romantic relationships. We feel that it is unfair for the cat or bi-nine lover to have to witness the dog person's external, and often loud, manifestation of anger, and advise that the dog individual be left alone until this period of rage subsides. (Incidentally, it should be noted that as unpleasant as explosive anger can be, the positive aspect to expressing anger so openly is that there's little hidden or repressed rage that will ultimately wreak havoc later in your relationship. This way, at least it can be dealt with head-on.) While dog men and women begin to realize that it's counterproductive for their lover to see them in the midst of their rage, cat and bi-nine individuals should learn the importance of articulating their anger. Understand that the *healthy* expression of anger is vital if you want real depth and honesty in your relationship, a lesson all cat, dog, and bi-nine people should strive to learn.

The second most frequent grievance involving dissatisfaction with dog lovers involves their legendary sloppy nature. If we could count the number of bi-nine, and especially cat, individuals who have expressed their horror at the slovenliness of dog people, you would be flabbergasted. As one cat man we interviewed recently stated, "How can Tammy *even exist* in such a mess? When we go to her apartment, I immediately become claustrophobic, my allergies act up. And I can't help but experience severe anxiety about what will happen if we ever move in together. What's a fastidious feline to do, anyway?"

What's a fastidious feline to do, indeed! Remember how upset Felix Ungar used to get at Oscar in The Odd Couple? Oscar was the poster boy for dog slovenliness— messiness seemed to exude out of him, and it drove Felix to become even more of an anal-retentive hypochondriac than he already was. The truth is that if Felix couldn't convert Oscar to his neat and orderly ways, you won't be able to change your dog lover slob into an organized canine. It's simply not in the canine's nature, so don't waste your energy, patience, or time. However, it is possible to negotiate boundaries with them, so insist that all shared spaces, such as the kitchen, living room, and bathroom, be kept free from their clutter and mess. If you'll be sharing an apartment with your canine love, getting two bedrooms, as well as two separate bathrooms, is simply a necessity. With this strategy, it will be easier to persuade them that it's okay if their room resembles a pigsty, but that their pigpenlike ways are absolutely limited to that room only.

The third complaint voiced by many cat and bi-nine people we interviewed concerned the lack of boundaries dog people sometimes have between their public and private life. For instance, Jackie infuriated her boyfriend, Troy, by inviting co-workers and casual friends along to their first anniversary dinner. "Look, I thought it was a bit strange when you invited a dozen people to vacation with us in Mexico," Troy complained, "but this is just too much! Anniversary dinners, by their very nature, are meant to be *intimate!*" Not for Jackie. Since she subscribes to "the more the merrier" school of thought, she genuinely had trouble understanding what Troy was so upset about.

Unlike most bi-nine and cat people, dog people, more often than not, have less rigid boundaries between different spheres in their life. They often don't differentiate between work and home, and usually end up bringing their work home, taking their kids to the office, and having co-workers as close friends. For cat people, this way of living is appalling since they insist on exercising rigid boundaries between their work and their personal lives. If you are currently upset by your dog lover's lack of ability to differentiate between these different spaces, you need to explain in tremendous detail exactly what you'd like changed—and that's the easy part! Remember, dog people respond to bluntness and honesty, so don't pussyfoot around attempting to give subtle and tactful reasons why their behavior is driving you crazy. We should warn you that the real challenge will be for your dog lover to appreciate your reasons for separating life into two distinct parts, when all along your significant other has happily considered it a unified whole.

Understanding Your Cat Lover

If you plan on becoming involved with a cat person, you better get used to three things right now. First, cat people will always hold themselves slightly apart from everyone in their lives, be it lovers, best friends, children, or parents. Second, since compartmentalization is a way of life for them, they will insist on separating their work life from their family, and they will sometimes even separate their family from their friends. Third, cat people can be a challenge to live with, especially regarding their neat, orderly, and "anal-retentive" ways, a term disgruntled dog people love to use against them. The truth is that even if you are the neatest dog person in the world, your cat lover will inevitably find some reason to complain about your housekeeping. Generally, these complaints will take the form of suggestions, like, "Wouldn't it be easier to keep the flour in a large mason jar, instead of the sloppy paper bag it comes in?" Naturally, this will have just followed a comment in which your cat lover has not only explained the advantages of real butter over margarine, but has also stressed how imperative it is that the butter be kept in the glass butter container in the fridge.

There is something about the maintenance of order, be it at home or at the office, that brings out that controlling streak in the feline personality. Cat people, for all their aloofness, will get highly involved when it comes to having things their way, and some of the things they insist on controlling are kitchens, bathrooms, and desks. Cat people, for all their roaming and commitment phobia, are exceptionally resistant to change in their actual living quarters. That's the one place where a single moved item can cause pandemonium. Even those deceptive cat people, who appear to be disorderly and almost doglike in their living environment, will balk at the imposition of someone else's notion of order. Non-cat people are initially perplexed by this unexpected territorialism, and they expect felines to be as aloof about their homes and offices as they are about the people who reside and work in them. Wrong! All cat people know better than to tamper with another cat person's personal belongings or, God forbid, to move a piece of furniture without permission. Such transgressions border on an act of war in the average cat person's mind.

So then, how do you live with these overly fastidious individuals? We suggest a simple guideline. When you begin cohabiting with a cat person, create a domestic comfort zone by initially agreeing with all their housekeeping and decor decisions. Over time, slowly suggest or introduce new elements and methods by first complimenting your cat person on his or her selection, presenting your addition as the perfect complement. This might arouse some suspicions, but your friendly, helpful, and innocent demeanor will emphasize your sincerity and should bring out their more generous side. Remember, just because cat people are suspicious of compliments doesn't mean they don't like them. If this tactic proves fruitless, it means you have a particularly difficult feline and that you should consider divvying up the house. This means that the bedroom and den are yours to do with as you wish, while the kitchen, bathroom, and living room belong to your lover. The decor might end up looking somewhat schizophrenic but, trust us, it's better than having arguments about something fundamentally unchangeable—basic differences in your characters, that is.

Next, let's talk briefly about your cat person's aloofness. Cat people, it must be accepted, are simply not as forthcoming or extroverted as dog or bi-nine people. You see, for typical cat people, solitude is golden, people are a distraction, and there is nothing they love as much as the company of their own minds. An ideal vacation for them is going to the beach, taking a leisurely stroll, and reading a thrilling novel in the sun for five hours, alone. They love going to concerts, hiking, and watching movies, alone. In fact, any hobby cat people have will probably be done by themselves at least half of the time. We knew one cat woman, for instance, who was an avid tennis player and loved practicing for hours with an automatic ball server. When people would offer to hit the ball opposite her, she would look at them bewildered, wondering why on earth she'd have any interest in doing that.

Initially, your cat lover's obsessive need for privacy can be a difficult thing for dog people and bi-nines not to take personally. Many a dog person has suffered, thinking they've done something wrong and that their cat lover's withdrawal is a sign of rejection. Truly, those cat people who cannot articulate their need for privacy risk alienating their loved ones, and dog people and bi-nines will accuse them of indifference or, worse yet, may use a phrase (often used in therapy) that drives them crazy: "You are with-holding!" Naturally, this type of accusation only makes the situation worse, resulting in the alienation of two people who might really care for each other.

Once you understand that your cat person is not, by any means, excluding you from activities, life can become much more blissful. Cat people need to recharge their interpersonal battery with private time and, believe it or not, they can actually be the most charming and guest-friendly people in the world, as long as they have the right balance of privacy and socializing. By the way, when two cat people get together, the situation can be equally diffi-cult. They may understand each other's need for privacy; however, if they fail to synchronize "togetherness time," they will compromise the nature of their emotional and romantic life, which will result in a relationship where neither lover's needs get met. Therefore, cat lovers must also make a conscious effort to reconnect with their cat person partner at least once a day.

When it comes to the issue of compartmentalization, things can be equally challenging for dog and bi-nine peo-ple. Cat people are notorious for keeping things and people apart, and a positive side effect of this is that your cat per-son can separate work from romance and home life. You will seldom compete with the office for attention when on vacation with your cat lover, nor will you have to worry that they'll invite the kids and in-laws along on your second honeymoon. If cat people do one thing right, it's prioritizing.

However, there's also a downside to keeping everything separate. Sometimes when you want to invite Katy, Bob, Sue, and your old high-school friend Ray for a picnic and jazz concert in Central Park, your cat lover will flatly refuse to accompany you. They'll say things like, "Katy's a bore, Bob's a control freak, Sue's a whiner, and Ray is tone-deaf. Sounds like the picnic from hell." Cat people hate being in situations where they see potential conflict. What they can't see, and what you must invariably help them understand, is that just because people are different, doesn't mean that an event has to be socially unpleasant. This is where a sociable and outgoing dog person or bi-nine can really make a difference. If trained well, your cat lover might not only come to admire your skill in handling Katy, Bob, and Sue, but he or she will also begin to trust your sense of fun and manage to relax and enjoy the music—even if Ray is never able to distinguish Thelonius Monk from John Coltrane.

Understanding Your Bi-nine Lover

Bi-nines, you might as well know: Cat and dog people are sick and tired of your so-called superiority complex. As

Like Cats and Dogs

Skip coolly said to his cousin, "Look, we all know you bi-nine men and women are highly gifted—if only because *you* keep telling us—but don't think you're the only special people on this planet." As unfortunate as it is, bi-nine people as a whole have developed a reputation for being patronizing with their cat and dog brethren in a number of ways, especially intellectually, artistically, and creatively. While most bi-nines will vigorously deny they have a patronizing bone in their body, cat and dog people swear by their egos that there's nothing quite like the experience of being squashed by a belittling bi-nine.

In all fairness to bi-nines, it should be clarified that while it may appear as though your bi-nine love is looking down on you as he or she starts to "lecture," sometimes it is in an effort to share something fascinating with the most important person in his or her life—you. Not everyone is convinced the bi-nine is being absolutely honest here, and it has been said that bi-nines sometimes seem to enjoy flaunting their knowledge to a greater extent than cat and dog people. However, we believe it's important to give your bi-nine lover the benefit of the doubt, if you possibly can.

But what happens when you know your bi-nine too well to believe they're innocently just telling you something? In other words, what should you do when your bi-nine lover really starts to hold forth on a topic, whether it's ancient Chinese civilizations or the unique character of fusion jazz from the late '60s. The truth, as we all know, is that "the lecture," could be on anything and will last for an indeterminate amount of time. As we see it, you have several options. You can (a) leave the room, (b) look your lover in the eye and say that you are hip to this subtle power game and that you don't appreciate it (this can be successful at least for the first few times), or (c) decide to fight fire with fire.

Should you choose option c, and we hope you will, all that is required is the following: Read up on some esoteric and obscure subject and, at some unsuspecting and public moment, give your bi-nine love a hearty and long-winded taste of the same medicine. For instance, we interviewed one dog man, Arthur, who, in the middle of a tour through the Museum of Natural History, casually turned to his bi-nine lover and spoke at tremendous length about the mating rituals of the rhinoceros beetle. Incidentally, he reported tremendous satisfaction at seeing his lover's eyes glaze over with boredom as he proceeded to hold forth on the subject, with painstaking detail, for over half an hour.

Another sore point with some cat and dog people concerns the bi-nine's complete disregard for convention. As we know, bi-nines are natural nonconformists, and bi-nine men and women have been known to dramatically claim that they would rather die than live an orthodox existence. Some cat and dog people have stated that they feel uncomfortable by the bi-nine's insistence on having to be different. In the words of Stacy, a cat woman, "My boyfriend, Carl, occasionally annoys me beyond belief. He has to do things to show how different or special or unique he is from everyone else. It's like he's out to prove this to me—or to himself. Like he's got a chip on his shoulder or something."

In order to get to the bottom of Stacy's complaint, we have to put it in the context of her relationship with Carl. For instance, while her comment indicates that Carl appears to be insecure about *not* being different from the crowd, it is also necessary to take into account that Stacy is a cat woman who relishes playing by the rules and doing the socially appropriate thing. Therefore, in Stacy's mind, anyone who strives to be different is somehow problematic. Obviously, this puts her comment in an entirely new light.

Indeed, many dog and cat people, without consciously realizing it, are staunch supporters of the status quo, and their prickly reactions to the nonconformist bi-nine can often sound a great deal like Stacy's reactionary response. In this matter, we feel we simply have to rush to the bi-nine's defense and urge cat and dog individuals to respect, and maybe even appreciate, the fact that their bi-nine lover is different. You have to admit, this is part of the reason why you were so attracted to your bi-nine love in the first place!

Understanding Your Cat, Dog, or Bi-nine Lover

We've all heard the saying, If it's catnip you're in search of, look no further than a bi-nine—they're sure to have some. It's no secret that a disproportionate number of bi-nines are interested in experimenting with different substances. It's also no secret that many dog and cat people can be highly critical, and a tad moralistic, about the bi-nine bias toward this type of experimentation. While it's not our place to denigrate the bi-nine and preach the virtues of a substance-free existence, we feel it's our duty to urge cat and dog people to explore the reasons why their bi-nine love may be a controlled-substance user.

First of all, the fact that bi-nine children are forced to mature in a cat-and-dog centered society is a jarring and painful reality. As one articulate bi-nine, Toni, told us, "Do you have any idea what it's like to grow up and only see images of cat and dog individuals? It's terrible for your self-esteem and really self-negating to not find *any* representation of yourself in society....It makes you feel like you don't exist, like you're crazy." Toni explained how easy it was to go from feeling alone and isolated to experimenting with various forms of catnip in order to ease the pain. Now she feels it has become a way of life and claims that it can alleviate her psychic pain in an altogether unique and effective way. Toni's lover, Pat (a hearty dog person), claims that understanding bi-nine history helps to make sense of Toni's complex relationship with mind-altering drugs, and while Toni and Pat are still trying to come to terms with their different attitudes, they've begun to discuss the issue in an informed, mature, and responsible way.

Fortunately, more and more bi-nines are asserting their identity publicly and are proud of being different from the status quo. This has had an amazingly beneficial effect on the bi-nine Generation X'ers, since they feel empowered by finally having their own role models.

CHAPTER 8

Cat and Dog
Breed Preferences

It's no surprise that there are undeniable differences between cat and dog owners. However, would you believe that there are also substantial differences between people who own one breed of cat or dog versus another? This section helps you get a cursory understanding of these differences and may even assist you in comprehending your pet and people selections better. After all, human relationships are merely a reflection of your feelings about your pets.

Like Cats and Dogs

Cat owners usually do not want to be smothered by their pets or overburdened by the responsibilities of pet ownership. They do not want to spend hours in the park exercising their pets, nor do they want the disorder and chaos that a bounding one-year-old retriever invariably brings into the well-ordered home. The average cat owner prefers an animal that is fastidious, content to be left alone, and easy to maintain. Essentially, cat owners see themselves as people, and the cat as an animal. They may appear less obviously involved with "the animal"—and more aware of their own limitations regarding the amount of time and energy they can realistically devote to their pet.

Dog owners, on the other hand, are the polar opposite. They envision their animals as little people, relishing being smothered, protected, and pounced on by their eighty-pound St. Bernard. They value loyalty and devotion in an animal, will refer to themselves as "Mummy" and the animal as "baby," and in general will show pictures, asserting to other dog owners and parents the superiority of their particular animal and its breed. Interestingly, unlike cat owners, dog owners are more likely to buy a 'trendy' animal, such as a dalmatian, without necessarily knowing a great deal about the breed. Dog owners believe their animals are their children and welcome the messy, chaotic four-legged bundles of joy into their lives. Frequently, they treat the breeder like an adoption agency and if, God forbid, the dog gets sick, they will require as much consolation and care from the vet as the dog itself. They also tend to enjoy socializing at the dog run, beaming like first-time parents at a PTA meeting.

Cats

Persian Cats

Individuals who own these creatures are generally considered real cat people and are known to cherish their animal's placid demeanor and exotic beauty. On the whole, Persian cats sport an almost ornamental appeal and certainly enhance the look of a lushly decorated apartment.

Siamese Cats

These rambunctious and friendly creatures can belong to either cat or dog people. Their highly interactive nature makes them palatable to the more doglike cat people, as well as the more catlike dog people. Slightly on the neurotic side, these felines tend to become jealous of their owner's new lovers or friends. It is said that this quality may appeal to people who need to feel wanted.

Burmese Cat

The Burmese cat owner is often as quiet and reserved as the animal itself. Marked by its luxuriant deep gray-blue coloring, the Burmese has an almost regal and dignified manner. In most cases, you'll find this feline by the side of many a fastidious, refined, and cultured cat person.

Abyssinian Cat

Extraordinarily doglike and active in its demeanor, this animal is often a dog substitute for dog people who are unable to keep a dog due to space and time limitations. Affectionate and playful, people with Abyssinians spend a great deal of time interacting with their animal, doting on them as on a long-lost child.

American Shorthair Cat

This cat is a wild card adopting either a dog or cat persona and may be wild or docile. What you can count on, though, is that the owner is a bonafide cat person as well as a huge cat fan. Open-minded and accepting, these owners are risk takers who are prepared to love their American short-hair in all of its manifestations despite its disposition.

Dogs

Shih Tzu

This small lion is reminiscent of a cat and is very appeal-ing to cat people in denial. Loyal and relatively small with a big and courageous personality, they are ideal for people who don't mind high-maintenance personalities since grooming is a vital part of owning this dog. It is rumored that some dog people, who are showy or ostentatious, particularly covet these creatures for their winning dog-show reputations. It is amusing to note that some shih tzu owners are as aloof and distant with new people, as the dog itself.

Retrievers (Golden & Labrador)

This is the ultimate dog person's dog—warm, friendly, patient, affectionate, gentle, and eager-to-please, these canines frequently embody many of the characteristics their owner's possess. Show us a person with a retriever, and we'll show you someone who loves nature, is generous, and is open about showing and receiving affection.

Yorkshires

These dog owners seek the ultimate accessory, a living one. Yorkshire owners enjoy the feeling of unequivocal power that possession of a toy dog gives them. Some cat owners find them catlike because of their size, but the Yorkshire personality is so dynamic that most dog-identified cat people usually choose a quieter or more lethargic breed. Essentially, people choose Yorkshires because their size allows them to be constant companions—in hotels, on planes, even in purses.

Cocker Spaniels

People attracted to cocker spaniels usually seek an audience. Enamored by the devoted and adoring nature of their pets, they use their animals to enhance their own sense of being valued in the world. It is fascinating to note that an unusually large number of performers and artists own these fastidious and stubborn little animals, and rumor has it that the owners are as high maintenance as the cocker spaniels themselves!

Rottweiler

People who have rottweilers, be they cat or dog people, are said to be invested in their image. These individuals enjoy the correlation between their own image and that of the dog as being protective, powerful, and dominant. Since they perceive outsiders as potential threats, owning a rottweiler substantially increases their sense of safety and control over their environment. It's not surprising, then, that these people are said to be especially guarded in the beginning of new relationships.

CHAPTER 9

Paw to Paw: The Path to Interspeciel Harmony: Why Can't We All Just Get Along?

HIGH MAINTENANCE	LOW MAINTENANCE	MIDDLE MAINTENANCE
Dogs	Dog People	Bi-nine People
Cat people	Cats	

Like Cats and Dogs

Our most frequently asked question, not surprisingly, is, Where is the right cat person, dog person, or bi-nine for me? In order to find your true cat, dog, or bi-nine lover, it becomes essential not only to understand what manner of species *you* are, but also to consider how compatible you are emotionally and romantically with these three different species.

For instance, as you know, cat people are notorious for being reserved, inscrutable, strategic, and self-sufficient to a fault. If you value communicating openly and easily with your lover, think twice before giving your heart to a feline. On the other hand, if you're positively intrigued by the passion and mystique inherent to cat men and women, perhaps a relationship with them is exactly what you need.

If you're hankering for an extroverted, friendly, and affectionate partner, dog people may be your speed. Still, think carefully, since virtually all these folks are tactless, native, and known as chatterboxes when being criticized by the cat brethren. It is true, however, that the energy, charisma, and enthusiasm of dog men and women have won them countless admirers.

The complex, often misunderstood, and idealistic bi-nines should be pursued by people searching for nonconformist and unconventional lovers. People who enjoy tradition, support the status quo, and define stability in orthodox terms will be offended by the naturally maverick and experimental bi-nine. Still, these visionary and unique individuals are often some of the most gifted and courageous people you'll ever know.

Another important factor to consider when deciding which species is perfect for you is whether you're searching for a high-, low-, or middle-maintenance lover. According to our chart at the beginning of the chapter, cat people are often considered high-maintenance because they are fastidious, aloof, and critical, while dog people tend to be a bit more casual, indiscriminately social, and carefree. John, the overly strategic cat man, epitomizes the high-maintenance nature of cat people, while Michael, the dog man, represents the lower-maintenance canine. Interestingly, actual dogs, on the other hand, are high maintenance, requiring a great deal of attention in the form of walking and grooming. Cats, however, are considered low maintenance because they thrive with relatively little human attention, use their own litter box, and frequently come and go as they please.

Additionally, the diagram helps us to understand why some cat people will choose to live with a dog or a dog person, and vice versa. This, not-infrequent phenomenon is accomplished by some cat people, dog people, and bi-nines out of a conscious desire for balance—a restoration of the yin and yang, if you will. Believe it or not, this kind of union can serve to highlight the best character traits of both the individual and the animal in question. Remember Derek, our betwixt and between bi-nine, who finally found his life partner in Joan, a cat woman? Stories such as Derek's aren't unusual, although they often involve much soul searching and an ability to compromise on the part of both people involved.

Keep in mind, too, that at different points in your life, you may be attracted to a different species of person. This is what happened with Chris, a bi-nine woman, who was first married to Charles, a cat man, and then had an affair with a classic dog man, Michael. As a young dog adolescent, you may be intrigued by mysterious cat people, while as a mature adult you find yourself more compelled by a bi-nine, and perhaps as an older individual you will crave the company of another dog person like yourself.

Our research suggests that apart from compatibility, the willingness of the individuals in question to be flexible and open to the unique challenges of an interspeciel or intraspeciel romance is crucial to the success of any relationship.

One last word of advice in your quest for love and friendship: Never ever compromise your respective cat, dog, and bi-nine values. Remember, no matter what, *you're* the pick of the litter.

Dear Readers,

We would like to invite you to submit your stories and anecdotes about cat, dog, and bi-nine personality types to us. Since this is still a relatively unexplored area, we believe that your observations would enrich our research in this psychosociological field.

For instance, let us know what happened to you on your last date with a dog man. What innovative techniques did you come up with to cope with your bi-nine son during adolescence? Why are you convinced that your girlfriend is the quintessential cat woman? And what does it mean for you to be a dog person with distinct bi-nine tendencies?

Please write, we'd love to share your insights with all those cat, dog, and bi-nine people out there.

Address:
Tanya McKinnon and Gayatri Patnaik
c/o Andrews McMeel Publishing
4520 Main Street
Kansas City, MO 64111